THE
GREAT
BLACK
DRAGON
FIRE

THE
GREAT
BLACK
DRAGON
FIRE
A Chinese Inferno

BY

HARRISON E. SALISBURY

LITTLE, BROWN AND COMPANY
BOSTON   TORONTO   LONDON

FIRST EDITION

The photographs in this book are the work of Xinhua News Agency
photographer Zhou Quo, PLA photographer Qiao Tianfu,
and Harrison E. Salisbury.

Library of Congress Cataloging-in-Publication Data

Salisbury, Harrison Evans, 1908–
    The Great Black Dragon fire : a Chinese inferno / by Harrison E.
Salisbury. — 1st ed.
        p.   cm.
    ISBN 0-316-80903-9 : $17.95
    1. Forest fires—China—Heilungkiang Province.   I. Title.
SD421.34.C6S25   1989
634.9′618′095184—dc19   88-34633
                                                              CIP

10   9   8   7   6   5   4   3   2   1

Designed by Robert G. Lowe

RRD VA

PRINTED IN THE UNITED STATES OF AMERICA

For Commander Ge Xueling,
former mayor Wang Zhaowin,
and all the other brave men and women
who fought the great Black Dragon fire

Contents

List of Maps

Acknowledgments

THIS ACCOUNT could not have been written without the generous aid and assistance of many Chinese, most notably those of General Yang Shangkun, now president of China, who personally arranged for me to visit the Heilongjiang Forest fire area as part of my larger project of examining the new policies and developments in China under the direction of Deng Xiaoping. Enormous firsthand help was rendered by my Chinese associates in this project: Zhang Wei and Liu Yadong of the Foreign Ministry, Cui Lie of the China Translation and Publishing Corporation, Wu Jun of the Press and Publications Administration, and Commander Ge Xueling of the Hinggan Forest Fire Control Center. I am also grateful to Jack Minor of the Canadian project; Scott Wade and Doug Hamilton of the Canadian embassy in Beijing; Alan Robock of the University of Maryland Meteorology Department; Horst Wagner, forestry specialist, World Bank, Washington, D.C.;

China specialist John S. Service; consulting forester Curtis Rand; Myron L. Heinselman, St. Paul, Minnesota, forest historical analyst; David Smith, Yale Forestry School; Mark C. Elliott, doctoral specialist, Manchu dynasty, Tokyo University; the Chinese Forestry Ministry and many of its officials and specialists; and too many citizens of Heilongjiang Province to name.

THE
GREAT
BLACK
DRAGON
FIRE

I

The Black Dragon

BY 10:30 in the morning of Monday, April 11, 1988, dust had so thickened the air of Beijing that a guard standing on the Tiananmen Gate of the Forbidden City could no longer see the Mao Zedong mausoleum in the center of the square only three hundred feet ahead of him.

By noon darkness enveloped the central boulevard of Chang-an Street. Office workers looking down from twenty-two-story windows saw only a yellow haze where the great boulevard ran below. Cyclists, faces swathed in scarves or handkerchiefs, dismounted and blindly stumbled through the murk. Trucks on the beltway slowed to a halt. Highways leading to Beijing began to resemble the Santa Monica Freeway on a foggy day, clogged with six- and ten-car collisions. Ambulances howled their way through the confusion. Scores were killed and injured. The sand-laden wind tore roofs from peasant huts, slammed billboards to the ground, blasted faces with what felt like buckshot, laid waste to greenhouses, killed cattle.

In the old days Beijing's spring was synonymous with dust, but nothing like this storm could be remembered. It went on and on, rising and falling in intensity for a fortnight, and spread over much of North China.

When Beijinger met Beijinger there was one word on their lips: Heilongjiang! The Black Dragon fire! Eleven months earlier China's worst forest fire in three hundred years — one of the worst in world history, if not *the* worst — had raged over the endless forests of the Black Dragon River, on the northeast border between China and Russia.

There had been instant concern that destruction of the "Green Sea," as the Chinese call the immense forests, would widen the great deserts to the north and east of the Chinese capital and bring back the deadly dust storms that had harassed the city since the middle years of the Ching dynasty.

These storms of the past had not been forgotten — "the yellow overhead, sifting downward in clouds of powder and covering everything, the whole atmosphere full of depression, tension, and suspense," as an American woman wrote in 1919. Or, as another wrote in 1951:

> The sky turns yellow. Within five minutes of the sky darkening and the first gust of wind your desk is grey and covered with grit. You can feel the coating of dust on your teeth. The streets are cloaked with clouds of dust and sand. It is almost impossible to breathe, let alone see. After a few minutes outdoors your face is black.

For more than two decades the storms had vanished. Now, in April 1988 — so people believed — the Black Dragon fire had brought them back. No matter what the experts said — and they insisted that the 1988 dust tornadoes could not have been caused by the Black Dragon fire — Beijing's citizens believed the opposite. The fire had begun to take its climatological toll. For a quarter century the great shelterbelt and irrigation works of the People's Republic had quelled the dust and the wind. Was it just coincidence that the Black Dragon forests burned in 1987 and the wind turned Beijing into an environmental nightmare in 1988?

Reassuring statements issued from the meteorologists. The press published calming stories. But Beijing eyes smarted from the dust that turned the sky yellow, Beijing faces ached from the wind-driven blasts of sand, Beijing lungs were racked with bronchial coughing. Beijing did not believe the scientists. To those who experienced the Beijing spring of 1988 it hardly seemed improbable that the Black Dragon fire might, as some had predicted, accelerate the desertification of Northeast China and produce not only regional distortions of weather but even displacement of long-standing patterns of global winds, with consequences for distant climes and continents.

The fire had started May 6, 1987, in one of the most remote corners of China, Manchuria's Greater Hinggan Forest (Da Hinggan Ling in Chinese). This forest sprawls for four hundred miles along China's northern frontier with the Soviet Union, roughly following the line of the Heilongjiang River, as the Chinese call it, which translates as the Black Dragon. (The river is known to the western world by its Russian name of Amur.)

Before I went to China in August 1987 I had seen a notice in the *New York Times* about the fire, enough to suggest that a major catastrophe might have occurred. When I got to Beijing I quickly learned that the catastrophe was of dimensions far greater than I had imagined.

In recent years I had spent a great deal of time in China. In 1983 and 1984 I had carried out a major project, writing an account of the Long March of Mao Zedong and his Communist Red Army, a six-thousand-mile trek in 1934–35. I retraced the full route of the march through the western and northwestern backcountry and interviewed scores of survivors, as well as most of the top leadership of China, all of them participants in the march. Now I proposed to write a book about what I called China's New Long March, the struggle led by Deng Xiaoping to put China on the road to modern high-tech society after the trauma of the Cultural Revolution and Mao's last years.

It struck me that if the Black Dragon fire had been as bad as I had heard, it would place a new and heavy burden upon China's already laden shoulders as she struggled toward a new epoch.

It was not easy to get the necessary permissions to take a first-hand look at the area of the fire. No western correspondents had been permitted to visit the site of the fire, along China's most northern frontier, a region closed to Chinese and foreign travel, a sensitive military defense zone where security comes first and ordinary travel is nonexistent.

But after some discussion and my strong argument that only by understanding the handicaps that China had to overcome could one evaluate the difficulties of the New Long March, permission came down to visit the fire zone and talk to those who had fought the fire or been its victims.

Even after I had secured permission to inspect the northern forests there were difficulties. Harbin, capital of Manchuria, is a day and a half by train from Beijing, northeast about 700 miles. Another 350 miles north lies Jiagedaqi, gateway to the forest and the fire.

Today the Chinese no longer use the name Manchuria to describe the area where the forest is located. They simply call it Northeast China. The southern part of the region is highly industrialized, including big cities like Harbin; Shenyang (the former Mukden); and China's Detroit, the auto metropolis of Changchun; as well as the great Daqin oil fields and broad agricultural plains.

The north is the land of the Hinggan Mountains, Lesser and Greater, endless forests of larch and pine and spruce and hemlock and birch, virgin forests like those that existed in northern Maine, Michigan, Wisconsin, and Minnesota before the timber lords cut them down and fire devastated what remained.

The Hinggan forests stretch without break to the Black Dragon River and across the river into Siberia, broad expanses of conifers spreading southeast into northern Korea and westward to a point slightly east of

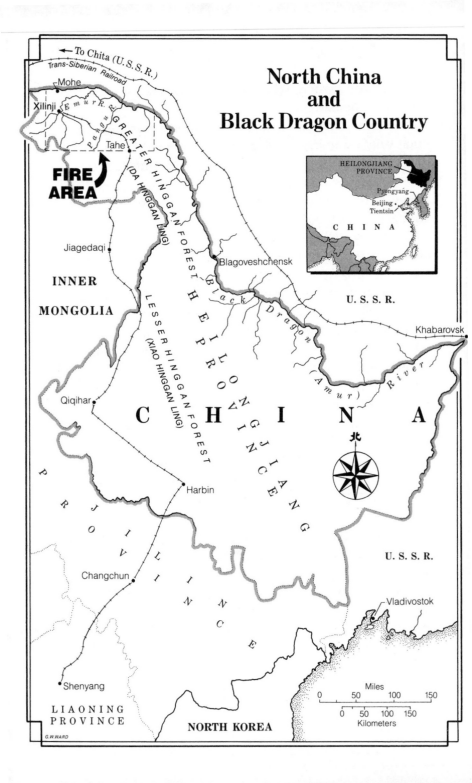

Chita, in Siberia. To the south they cross the northern reaches of Mongolia into China.

The Black Dragon River bisects the forest from west to east, dividing it into Russian and Chinese segments. On the Russian side the Trans-Siberian Railroad, the world's longest, roughly parallels the forest. No Chinese railroad traverses the forest, but in recent years a spur has been built to accommodate timbering operations on the southern edge of the Greater Hinggan Range. This spur runs from the gateway at Jiagedaqi north and west to the big forest center of Xilinji.

A crude American equivalent of the Black Dragon country would be a virgin tract of conifers extending from Maine west to Detroit, on both sides of the Canadian border, with the St. Lawrence bisecting the green mass and Washington, D.C., approximating Beijing. The train trip from Washington to Portland, Maine, would equate with that from Beijing to Jiagedaqi.

The great forest made up of the two Hinggan branches represents the largest stand of virgin conifers in the world, a priceless mass of beautiful timber five hundred miles long and three hundred or more miles wide. No other such a pool of conifers exists; in fact, the Chinese-Soviet forest is the largest single timber stand in the world. No North American forest comes close to it. This stand constitutes (or did before the fire) about one third of China's total forest reserves.

When I inquired at the Forestry Ministry, in Beijing, about the fire, they told me that more than 3 million acres of China's reserves — at least one sixth and possibly one fifth of her total timber — had been destroyed. But this was not all. Almost simultaneous with the

Chinese fire had been two fires on the Soviet side. From satellite photos the Chinese estimated that the Soviet fires were three or possibly four or five times larger than the Chinese. If these estimates are correct (no Soviet statement has been made), it means a Russian loss of 9 million to 15 million acres, totaling a world loss in prime timber of as much as 18 million acres in a few days in May 1987.

All estimates about a conflagration of this order — so large that, like China's Great Wall, it could have been seen from the moon — are necessarily approximations. I could find no forest specialist who would try to assess what percentage of the world's conifer reserves had been destroyed. It may have been one tenth. It may have been more. Governor Hou Jie, the boss of Heilongjiang Province, where most of the damage occurred, a burly man more accustomed to escorting fellow drillers from Edmonton or Texas around the Daqin oil fields than to forests, calculated the amount of timber ruined at 52 million cubic yards, worth possibly $3.3 billion. Another 20 million cubic yards was lightly damaged. At first it was thought that half this would be reclaimed, leaving a loss in timber of $500 million. A year later it was clear that the figure would be considerably greater because of slowness in cutting and rapid spread of infestation. Property damages were estimated at another $150 million in homes, buildings, machinery, equipment, and furnishings. The total runs to $4 billion or $5 billion. This takes no account of the losses in the Soviet fires, which would add many more billions. There were about 220 deaths and 250 seriously burned and injured in China.

Like most fires, the Black Dragon pursued a random, unpredictable course. Driven by winds of more than 60 miles an hour, it rushed down on towns and villages with a wall of flames sometimes sixty to one hundred feet high. But occasionally it leapt over a half mile or more, leaving the land unharmed, only to burn to a black crisp the next forest segment.

The area of devastation was almost the size of New England, nearly thirty thousand square miles of forest, roughly the size of Vermont, New Hampshire, Massachusetts, and Connecticut. An area as large as Scotland was turned into a dark mass of black stumps and carbon cinders. The fire's swath was as long as the shuttle flight from New York to Boston and wider than Long Island at Westhampton.

There is no record of a fire of such magnitude in China, not in the meticulous annals of the twenty-four dynasties. World forestry does not document such a conflagration. The only comparable description is that in the biblical account of the Apocalypse. The scale of Black Dragon was so grandiose that silviculturists and environmental experts could not escape thinking beyond regional changes to continental transformations in spheres of growth, species, wind, temperature, and erosion, to fertile fields turning to desert, as has already happened in Northwest China, to new patterns of climate, wind and water erosion.

Before the fire the Chinese had delighted in talking of the forest as "a sea of green" or as "the Forest Ocean." Indeed, the hotel at Jiagedaqi, administrative center for the great forest, bears the name Lin Hai, Forest Sea.

I found it hard to believe — I still do — that a catastrophe so great had gone almost unnoticed in the west. Even a year after the fire, specialists in the United States possessed only bits and pieces of information about it. Not since the famine of 1929–30, in which six million Chinese starved to death north of the Yellow River and were mentioned in no more than a few paragraphs in the *New York Times*, had so great a tragedy been ignored by so many.

All the fires — the Chinese fire in the Greater Hinggan Mountains and the Russian fires to the north — occurred in the watershed of the Black Dragon River. This great stream, the third largest in Siberia, a majestic water course roughly 2,000 miles long that drains a basin of 710,000 square miles and empties into the Sea of Japan, captured my imagination. Why was it called the Black Dragon? Dragons in the fairy stories I had read as a child were fearsome creatures, breathing flame and smoke. Might there not be some connection in the minds of the people living along the Black Dragon's littoral between the dragon that had given the river its name and the terrible fire that had devastated the land of the Black Dragon?

Once in the Black Dragon country I began to question people about the river's name. I did not get very far. The river had always been called Black Dragon, people said. They knew nothing more. They were down-to-earth forest workers, engaged in coping with the aftermath of the great fire that had destroyed their world. They did not give much thought to inquiries about legends or superstitions. One man told me that he thought there was a myth about the struggle of a

Black Dragon and a White Dragon. The Black Dragon won and became the lord of the river. The White Dragon lost and scurried down to South China to take up residence in a large lake that still bore his name. I searched in vain for an old sage who might tell me of an ancient prophecy that the Black Dragon was jealous of the forest and if crossed would rise up in anger and destroy it.

One day I was talking with a group of survivors of the fire. They were telling me how the fire had roared down on them faster than a man could run, even faster than a truck could jolt over the rutted forest roads. I heard of terror and tragedy, of wives lost and children burned to cinders, but nothing about dragons.

Finally a People's Liberation Army commander began to describe how the fire bore down "like a red sea wave" at a speed that he estimated at 40 miles an hour.

"Did it sound like an express train?" I asked, repeating a comparison that had been offered by a railroad worker. No, said the officer, "it was more serious than that. It sounded like an artillery barrage. It was the sound of terror."

I asked the others of what the sound had reminded them. A factory worker said, "It was like a thousand machine tools." Another said it resembled "a tornado of fire." Did anyone else have an idea? There was a considerable pause. Then a young forester hesitantly said: "Well, I guess you could say it sounded like the roar of a dragon."

The roar of a dragon. That was the answer I had been fishing for. I thanked the young man. The Black Dragon of the river, I suggested, had turned on the people. I was quite pleased with my persistence until I began to research the subject and found that in China the dragon possesses a personality quite at odds with the dragon slain by Saint George. The Chinese dragon is benign, even good-hearted. True, he is imperial, the symbol of empire. Both the Ming and the Qing dynasties fought under the banner of the dragon. But he is not evil. He is, to the contrary, the god of water and rain. He protects crops. He averts famine and flood.

In the twelve-year Chinese cyclical calendar the dragon year follows that of the rabbit and precedes that of the snake. The year 1988 was a Year of the Dragon, and its advent filled Chinese newspapers with dragon lore. I read of a scholar who advanced the hypothesis that the Forbidden City, with its lakes and canals, is modeled on the architecture of the dragon. I found that the dragon year was a year of joy and festivals — processions of wonderful snaky paper dragons operated by hidden dragon men. Dragon kites were flown on the Day of Pure Brightness, April 4. In June and July there were races of dragon boats.

Clearly the Chinese dragon had little in common with the dragon of my imagination. Yet as I talked with those stricken by the fire my mind began to shift to my original notion. The Black Dragon had not fulfilled his folkloric role. He had not brought rain and snow when rain and snow were needed. More and more I heard talk of dragon wind and dragon fire. Finally someone gave me a poem, "An Ode to the Heroes of the Fire-Fighting." It was published in a collection put out by the Popular Art Center of the Hinggan prefecture, at Jiagedaqi. It began:

A dragon of fire, running wild through the forest,
Setting every tree ablaze and touching off bright torches
Like a monster starved for a century,
Destroying everything;
Like a rocket the fire raced everywhere,
Giving vent to rage — rage pent up for thousands of
   years.

II

"A Sound Like Shouting Voices"

THE BLACK DRAGON COUNTRY now seems so remote and peaceful that it took me a long time to understand what a land of fire and strife it has been.

Fridtjof Nansen, the great Norwegian explorer, passed through this territory nearly one hundred years earlier. The Russians were just completing the Trans-Siberian Railroad, on their side of the river, and Nansen was convinced that this would be "the land of the future." The forests were endless. A great Siberian trader named Skidalski was already exporting valuable Korean cedar via Vladivostok.

Nansen explored both the Russian and Chinese watersheds of the Black Dragon River and later recalled that he was seldom out of sight of smoke from burning trees and savannas. The forest fires were touched off by carelessness of the masses of workers constructing the railroad and by sparks from wood-burning locomotives. The fields and meadows were burned by settlers whose fires escaped into the forest and destroyed thousands of acres.

"We now see smoke on every side; grass and forest are being burned indiscriminately," Nansen wrote. "The air is entirely filled with it, and the hills are shrouded in thick grey mist. The sun is red as blood. It is a fantastic scene with the rapidly increasing twilight and the red, smoke-filled sky."

Summer, Nansen reported, was often wet, but fall and spring were dry with winds so strong they left forest patches twisted with fallen trees. He met a merchant who had raced ahead of a fire in his troika, escaping the pursuit by driving into a pond up to the horses' necks. The wind, Nansen said, made a sound "like shouting voices."

From the deck of a river steamer Nansen saw unbroken stands of timber, great pillars of rock, and sunny, flower-strewn meadows waiting for the plow of civilization.

The forests were so vast that no one ascribed any value to them. They were inexhaustible, like air and water. Czarist law entitled all Siberians to "use the forest for their needs free and gratis." The Chinese had no law of the forest. People came and went and did as they pleased.

This philosophy had already permitted the ravaging of western Siberia, and ambitious intruders were beginning to gnaw at the edges of the incomparable Black Dragon country. No one took it upon himself to protect either the forest or the animal riches of ermine, sable, red and blue fox, mink, pine marten, lynx, bear, and the magnificent Siberian tiger. Some of the greatest fortunes in Russia and Manchuria were founded on the pelts of these precious beasts.

Nansen's impression of bucolic meadows, fields of northern buttercups, phalanxes of dark and silent larch and spruce, was deceptive. The struggle for these lands had gone on for centuries between the Russians and the Chinese. Now, during Nansen's time, the Japanese were eyeing them covetously.

Not until I entered the zone of the forest fire beside the Black Dragon River did I begin to grasp the real nature of this distant verge of empire. The Black Dragon had been a trigger line of imperial strife between the czars and the Manchus for three centuries. Now Russian and Chinese Communists watched each other warily across its dark waters.

Strife was hard to imagine as I gazed over a lazy sandbar to the quiet Russian village of Ignashino, not a mile away, where I saw cows grazing in a scrubby pasture, heard dogs barking and trucks racing their motors. Nor was there sign of tension in the sleepy riverside town of Mohe, sometimes called the Arctic village, where I stood staring at Soviet territory.

Three hundred and fifty years before there had been no Russians at the Black Dragon. The entire area was the fiefdom of the great Manchu warrior dynasty. In the early seventeenth century the Manchus, vigorous and powerful, rulers of all of Manchuria, eastern Siberia, and what are now the maritime provinces of Russia, seized the Dragon Throne in Beijing and became masters of all China. In those years there was no menace, no conflict, no frontier, at the Black Dragon River. All to the north and all to the south was ruled by the Manchu Chinese emperor.

But within a quarter century an obscure collision occurred. Russian adventurers were pushing east in search of gold and furs. A vanguard headed by an iron-fisted captain named Khabarov stumbled upon a village at Albazin, located at the conflux of the Emur and the Black Dragon rivers, a few miles east and north of where I stood on the riverbank at Mohe. Khabarov had no idea whose village he had encountered. The outpost had never heard of Russia. The two sides fought a blind fight and Khabarov won.

For thirty years skirmishing went on along the Black Dragon until the Manchus built a military road through the wilderness to the river, brought up thousands of troops, and imposed the Treaty of Nerchinsk on the Russians on August 27, 1689. This confirmed the Manchu emperor's right to his hereditary lands. All of the Black Dragon and the unknown marches to the north and east (there were no maps; no one knew where Siberia ended) went to China. The czar didn't care. His ideas of geography were also vague.

The treaty diverted Russia's thrust northward, away from Manchuria. Quiet descended on the Black Dragon country. The military road built by Emperor K'ang Xi fell into disuse. The *ostrog*, or fort, at Albazin was razed. Gradually the Chinese pulled back the divisions they had stationed to guard against the "long noses" (the Chinese regard all westerners as having Jimmy Durante noses). With the passing of years China's imperial power waned.

By the mid-nineteenth century China had lost the Opium War to Britain, and the Europeans, with Russia in the forefront, began to carve up the imperial dynasty. Russia seized the ancient Manchu heritage north and east of the Black Dragon. Japan would later flex its muscles, defeating China in a brief war toward the close of the century, and prepare to give the czar a taste of the same medicine. Tension had been rising on the Black Dragon and rose again when gold was discovered. A big strike in 1887 set off a Chinese Klondike stampede.

A short distance from Mohe, just ten miles south of the river on a small creek, I saw the remains of the Chinese gold rush at a fire-blackened nest of burned larch and scorched birch called Lao Guo. Here only the aspens with their yellow and green flags waved over the desolation wrought by the recent conflagration.

Once prospectors had flocked by the thousand to Lao Guo — Chinese, Russians, Manchus, Mongols, Tungusi, the native Er Lunchen tribe (still resident in the area), a few Japanese, and half a dozen Americans. By 1890 nearly eighteen thousand grams of gold made its way to St. Petersburg from the Black Dragon deposits. An equal amount or more went into Chinese hands, but how much got to the imperial treasury in Beijing is not known. The empress dowager Cixi, who presided over the last years of the Manchus, revived the old military post road through Lao Guo and sent her soldiers down it to collect what gold they could and bring it back to Beijing.

The Black Dragon country was rough and tough, like the American Wild West. Men took the law into their own hands. When gold was discovered on the Sheltuga, a small Black Dragon tributary in Chinese territory, some six thousand to twelve thousand prospectors streamed in. They set up their own "Free Republic" with Wild Bill Hickok constables and hanging judges on horseback. The "republic" carried on for three or four years until Chinese regular troops were sent in to take over.

Hundreds of prostitutes had followed the gold seekers into the remote mining camps. In 1986 a Chinese film crew making a documentary called *The Golden Road* found the graves of several hundred women in a special cemetery for prostitutes outside the Lao Guo mine. Flasks in which their ashes had been preserved lay strewn across an overgrown field.

Today's miners at Lao Guo and prospectors panning for gold along the Black Dragon tributaries still follow the lore of the Gold Road. They carve the word *jin* (gold) on their picks and shovels. They will not speak the Chinese words for "empty" or "hollow." They do not permit women in their diggings.

At the peak of activity there may have been a hundred thousand prospectors spread over the river basin in Russia and China. Now a handful of prospectors still pan for gold, and a mine or two like Lao Guo (Post 32 on the Gold Road) and Xikuoqi (Post 33, just over the border in Inner Mongolia) are still active.

Lao Guo came close to destruction in the great fire. Its refinery burned, and the barracks, offices, and outbuildings were charred. A laconic miner named Wang Yiling bosses a force of seventy-six. He recovers about 380 grams of gold a day with a hydraulic dredge, about

10,000 grams a year. He showed me a day's take of gold dust (no nuggets in the gravel he screens) in a fine linen poke about the size of a Bull Durham bag. He ships the gold by truck. A policeman rides shotgun, armed with a submachine gun and a pistol. The gold goes to a nearby mine that did not lose its refinery in the fire.

The town of Mohe lay quiet in the autumn sunshine on the day of my visit in 1987. By a quirk of wind and fate it had come through the fire almost unscathed. But signs of tension on the frontier were not hard to find. Border troops in spit-and-polish uniforms carefully examined our papers at the checkpoint before allowing my escorts and myself to pass into Mohe. A monument to the PLA troops who keep twenty-four-hour watch on their Soviet counterparts across the river stood nearby with an inscription in the calligraphy of General (now President) Yang Shangkun, China's top military man. It read: "PLA Sentinels on the Northern Tip, June 20, 1984."

No foreigners — so I was assured — had visited the northern tip in recent times. The periphery of the frontier with Russia is closely controlled. Even during the great fire Chinese helicopters and planes avoided flying over the river or any Soviet territory.

Once there had been normal intercourse, with Russian and Chinese fishing boats side by side, Russians rowing across the Black Dragon to trade at the dusty little shops in Mohe, Chinese doing the same in Ignashino. There had been a fair amount of intermarriage of Chinese and Russians.

That had come to an end in the 1960s, when discord arose between Russia and China, especially in 1969 and thereafter, as the countries tottered on the brink of war. All contact was cut. Russian gunboats of the Amur River fleet roared down and capsized Chinese fishing vessels. Chinese stopped swimming in the river. Border trade was ended. Each side erected tall watchtowers to keep an eye on the other. The towers still stand there, and a Chinese companion delightedly told me that the Soviet tower was equipped with a videocamera. "They will be looking at your picture next week in Moscow and speculating what you are up to," he said.

The powerful loudspeakers that had blared insults across the river were now silent. The Soviet tanks that had paraded on the Ignashino waterfront long since had been withdrawn. The infantry detachment that once had scrambled ashore on the big sandbar in front of Mohe, firing machine guns wildly at a Chinese squad that wrestled some Russians to the ground, had vanished.

There was a small river freighter tied up on the Ignashino waterfront, and a couple of young men dug potatoes on the Mohe side. I thought I could see a few casual strollers on the Russian shore. If there were weapons aimed across the river, they were invisible.

Contact of a kind had been restored. Television aerials stood on most of the houses in Mohe, and I could see TV antennas on the Ignashino houses. The Chinese could watch Russian programs. "Very dull, too much talk" was the Chinese verdict. I was sure the Russians said the same of Chinese programs. But I could find no

Chinese who would admit having ever been on the Soviet side. The only Russian they could remember coming to their shore was a Soviet deserter who swam the channel in 1968. He was sent back. No Russian, the Chinese swore, now lived on their side. But I did see a Chinese with red hair, blue eyes, and Slavic face, a relic of the past, no doubt.

Official relations had also — in a way — been resumed. Not far from the river I was shown a rustic cottage behind a picket fence, the yard overgrown in weeds and light blue windflowers. At the cottage, on the Chinese national holiday, October 1, the Chinese border guards treated their Soviet counterparts to a feast, drunk down with quaffs of fiery *maotai*. Afterward the border guards strolled through Mohe, inviting their Russian guests to shop in the Chinese stores (conveniently stocked with scarce goods to demonstrate the good life on the Chinese side). On the Soviet holiday, November 7 — the anniversary of the Bolshevik Revolution — the process was repeated on the Russian side. The Soviet guards flew their flags at the riverbank as a signal of invitation, and the Chinese joined them for *zakuski* and vodka.*

The great fire did not touch Mohe town. But at its height no point was more threatened. Two arms of the

---

* In the latter half of 1988, with growing relaxation of Soviet-Chinese relations, small trade between Heilongjiang River towns was resumed for both Russians and Chinese. River traffic by both sides increased, and visits by Chinese to several Soviet river towns were followed by return visits by Russians. There was every expectation that within a few more months the river situation would return to pre-1960s status. Plans were being advanced for transmission of electric power from Soviet generators to Chinese plants across the river and other joint economic ventures.

Chinese fire leapt toward Mohe from the west, halting only a few miles away. And at night the people of Mohe saw the crimson glow of fires on Russian soil. Some Mohe officials got in their jeeps and jounced west along the banks of the Black Dragon on forest trails. The Soviet fire, as best they could estimate, was rushing toward the junction of the Black Dragon and the Ergun River, to the west. A finger of the Chinese fire had already penetrated almost to the Ergun at a place called Mangui, on the Inner Mongolian border.

If the Russian fire moved farther east and the Chinese fire farther west of Mohe, the Black Dragon River would be engulfed in flames from both sides and become a corridor of fire. This did not happen. But not far to the east, fire on both sides of the Black Dragon caused the Soviets to remove their Amur flotilla from the area.

The danger that fire would leap over the river was real. In this area the banks slope gently to the water. With tornado winds rising, only remarkable luck kept the Soviet fire from crossing to the Chinese side, and vice versa.

For all its history of conflict and tension, Mohe would be the only town I visited that bore no scar of the fire. A vision of this peaceful borderland would linger in my mind as I made my way through the wake of the Black Dragon fire.

III

A Brush Cutter

IN GREAT DISASTERS the nominal cause is often an act as trivial as that of Mrs. O'Leary's cow, which kicked over a lantern and started the Chicago fire of 1871. In China's Black Dragon fire it was an eighteen-year-old's need to earn 40 yuan, about $15, to buy a railroad ticket back home.

The eighteen-year-old was a well-built, broad-faced, rather handsome farmer named Wang Yufeng. He lived in Julong County, in Hebei Province, about 125 miles east of Beijing, and he had been spending the spring holiday with his cousin in Xilinji. It was time for him to go back home, and he didn't have the money.

On April 28, 1987, his cousin's wife ran into an old friend, Li Yi, in the railroad station. Li Yi was in charge of a tree-planting group at the nearby Gulian forest farm, one of the biggest and best timber-cutting operations in the Greater Hinggan Forest. The wife asked Li Yi if he could give Wang a job to earn the money for his ticket.

Jobs in the Black Dragon forest complex are hard for outsiders to come by, but Wang was in luck. Li Yi was short of hands. A lot of his workers — he was a brigade leader, a sub-boss — hadn't gotten back yet from the spring holiday. Li Yi would not have thought of giving Wang a permanent job, but he was happy to take him on as a temporary. Temporaries got low wages, no perks, and no security.

The day after the conversation at the railroad station, April 29, Wang went to work in the forest. This was against the rules, but no one paid much attention. A week later, May 6, Wang was assigned as a brush cutter to a tree-planting team of six. He was issued a model DC-3 cutter made by the Taizhou Forest Machinery Company of Jiangsu. It had been painted orange for visibility in the forest, but the paint had worn off. The cutter was gasoline-powered with a cutting blade at the end of a five-foot bicycle-tubing frame designed to be held tight against the body. The gasoline tank was a small cylindrical can attached to the frame. A pull cord started the motor. Except for being heavier, it was almost identical to an old American cutter.

How much instruction Wang had in the use of the machine is not clear, but it could not have been much. On the morning of May 6 he joined the team and walked with the five others down from the trim, modern headquarters complex on a dirt and gravel road for a little more than a mile before striking off across two hundred yards of muskeg to a line of trees. There he would cut brush, and the others would plant saplings and clear away forest debris. The DC-3 cutter could run for an hour and a half on a tank of fuel. Wang, as was the custom, had brought an extra tin of gasoline for a refill. He was not planning to work all afternoon, but he had enough gasoline to power the cutter until 3:00 P.M.

So far as anyone has discovered, the work went smoothly during the morning. The day was warm and pleasant. There had been little rain or snow for months, and already the forest floor was dry and tindery.

The team halted for a lunch break sometime around noon. After lunch the workers strolled back to their tasks. They were working at the edge of a broken clump of woods, visible from the main gravel road, which led to Xilinji. About half a mile in the other direction an access road curled up a small hill, at the top of which sat the Gulian forest headquarters. When I visited in September, four months after the fire, the savanna was waterlogged from summer rains, but on May 6 the tufted grass was dry.

Like all the forest farms the Gulian unit was a well-managed operation. There were strict rules for almost everything, including the handling of brush cutters. In Wang's case a good many of these rules were violated. Only trained personnel were supposed to run the cutters. The cutter was to be refueled only at the machine depot on a cement floor or in an area cleared of vegetation, such as a road or highway. The gas tank was not to be filled to the brim.

If Wang was aware of these requirements he paid no heed. With his fellow workers scattered over an area of several hundred yards, he took his spare can of gasoline and poured it into the fuel chamber of the cutter. He made a sloppy job of it, spilling gasoline over the frame of his cutter and onto the ground. He then pulled the starting cord. The spark instantly ignited the gasoline, and the cutter was enveloped in flames. The terrified Wang tried to pull it away to a safer area, but his efforts made things worse. The fire spread to the gasoline he had spilled on the ground. Tendrils of flame touched off the dry grass and raced over the open savanna and into the adjoining woods, a mixture of larch, white birch, and aspen. The half-dozen workers, Wang included, tried to beat out the flames, but they spread in all directions.

Had Wang worked the last one and a half hours of that afternoon as he had planned, he would have earned 2.10 yuan, about 75 cents. The cost of the fire caused by his clumsiness, in direct losses, was estimated by state investigators at 421 million yuan, about $150 million.

The spot where Wang's fire began was, when I saw it, a place of desolation, empty of such human signs as huts, houses, and landmarks. The landscape was much like the cutover, burned-over northern Minnesota of my youth, the forest ragged, tangled with burned and fallen timber, birches charred to a height of thirty feet, larch blackened tip to root, only the bright yellow banners of the aspen lighting the gloom. If you walked three hundred feet into this country on a cloudy day with neither sun nor shadow to tell you which direction was north and which south, you would be lost.

Gulian itself, the forest headquarters, was amazingly undamaged despite the loss of thousands of acres of prime forest and its entire stock of cut timber. Gulian is

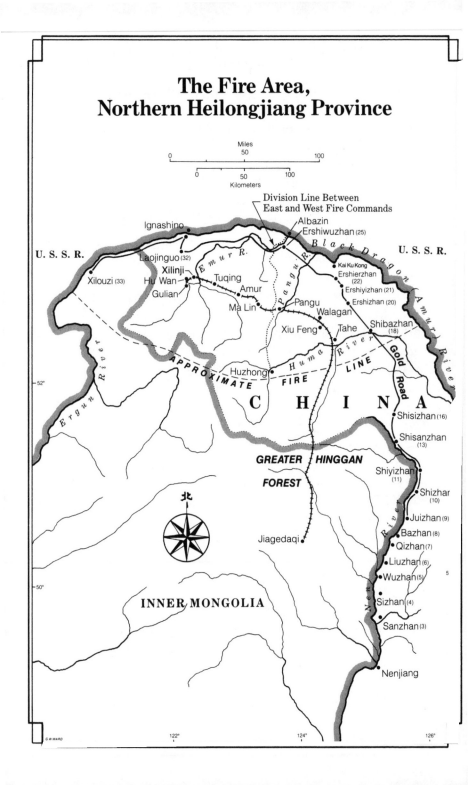

The Fire Area,
Northern Heilongjiang Province

Miles
0   50   100

0   50   100
Kilometers

Division Line Between
East and West Fire Commands

U. S. S. R.

U. S. S. R.

Ignashino

Albazin
Ershiwuzhan (25)

Black Dragon

Laojinguo (32)

Emur R.

Pangu R.

Kai Ku Kong
Ershierzhan (22)

Amur River

Xilinji
Hu Wan
Gulian

Xilouzi (33)

Tuqing
Amur
Ma Lin

Pangu

Ershiyizhan (21)

Ershizhan (20)

Xiu Feng

Walagan
Tahe

Shibazhan (18)

Gold Road

Huzhong

Huma River

FIRE   LINE

C H I N A

Ergun River

APPROXIMATE

52°

Shisizhan (16)

Shisanzhan (13)

GREATER   HINGGAN

Shiyizhan (11)

FOREST

Shizhar (10)

Juizhan (9)

Bazhan (8)
Qizhan (7)
Liuzhan (6)
Wuzhan (5)

Nen River

Jiagedaqi

5

Sizhan (4)

50°

Sanzhan (3)

INNER MONGOLIA

Nenjiang

北

G W WARD

122°

124°

126°

the most westward of the eight forest farms under the direction of the Xilinji Forest Bureau, which has jurisdiction over nearly 1.1 million acres of the Black Dragon River forest.

The highly successful Gulian farm was the largest in the area, employing about one thousand workers. Located on the spur railroad, it could ship directly with a minimum of trucking. Even in the bitter year of 1987 it shipped about 50,000 cubic yards of wood and in 1988 expected to be back at its 1986 level of 90,000. Each forest farm possessed a timber stand, trucks, forest equipment, machine shops, and sawmills.

The forests are state-owned, under the jurisdiction of the Forestry Ministry, in Beijing. Being so distant and self-contained, they have long constituted an independent kingdom, looking unkindly on outsiders and maintaining warm and close relations with the PLA, whose defense posts, artillery, anti-aircraft, and first-alert infantry detachments are scattered through the green recesses of the boundary forest.

Forest farms and forest bureaus sprawl across the expanse of the Black Dragon region from Inner Mongolia on the west far beyond Jiagedaqi, and from west of the river Emur at the edge of Mongolia to well east of the Huma River and Tahe.

Since, by good fortune, the blaze had started almost within sight of the Gulian headquarters, the alarm was quickly raised and forest workers streamed to the scene. At first the fire that Brush Cutter Wang started did not seem particularly dangerous. Fires along the fringe of the Hinggan Range have not been uncommon since the railroad arrived in the 1970s. Soon after the founding of the People's Republic of China, in 1949, a plan was devised to try to cut trees along the banks of the Black Dragon River and float them downstream for processing. But there were no roads, only forest trails to the river, and the scheme had to be abandoned because the government could not supply the cutters with food, gasoline, and equipment. A new plan was put together in 1965 only to be quickly abandoned by the Great Proletarian Cultural Revolution. Not until 1972 were the forest farms — that is, timber-cutting and -processing stations — set up, each assigned a large tract of forest that usually extended from the planned route of the railroad to the river. In 1974, with the railroad in place, timber operations on a large scale gradually got under way.

Fires along the right-of-way quickly began to plague the area. The railroad grades are steep. The Hinggan Mountains rise to peaks of five thousand feet and slope down gradually to the Black Dragon River. A north-facing forest, it is ideally situated for growth, while the Soviet forest across the river faces south. Double engines are needed to pull timber loads of twelve to fourteen flatcars. Brake shoes turn cherry red and spin off sparks, which set on fire the brush and trees along the tracks. Efforts to persuade train crews to halt at intervals and let the brakes cool down have had little success. The railroad has its concerns, the lumbermen theirs.

This kind of bureaucratic intransigence is typical in China. Bureaucrats do not readily yield their turf. It is one of the most stubborn problems with which Chairman Deng Xiaoping has had to contend. After the fire Canada shipped the Black Dragon Forest administration scores of preset fire detectors to be mounted in the forest. These detectors automatically transmit alarms on wireless frequencies in response to fire. The Forestry Ministry picked a clear frequency unused by anyone. After the alarms had been sent to Jiagedaqi, the PLA and Civil Aviation Administration objected to the frequency chosen by the ministry. The alarms had to be shipped back to Canada, reset, and returned, entailing a delay of months, simply to assuage bureaucratic pretensions.

But bureaucracy is not the only hazard to the magnificent stands of conifers, especially in the Lesser Hinggan Forest (or Xiao Hinggan Ling, in Chinese), to the south and east of the Greater Hinggan. This forest, originally all conifers, now is badly polluted with birch, aspen, and "junk" trees of no commercial value. It is sculptured by meadows and fields where peasants pasture cattle and sheep. Tribal herdsmen camp summerlong on the grasslands beside the foothills. Their campfires often spread into the dry meadow grass and shriveled muskeg, then up the mountain draws into standing timber.

The mountains are dotted in late summer and early autumn with mushrooms, especially the rare monkey's head, or *houtou*, a delicacy in Chinese markets. It brings 5 yuan a kilo, 75 cents a pound, in the forest towns but ten or more times as much in Beijing. Peasant pickers with their woven cedar baskets can, if lucky, pick six or seven pounds a day, a prince's ransom. Hundreds — thousands — descend on the Hinggans, defying every effort to control access. They camp for days or weeks, often leaving smoldering fires behind.

And then there are the gold prospectors. They wander in from all over China, sometimes with permits, sometimes without. The forests are closed to outsiders during peak fire-hazard times in the spring and autumn, but all the vigilance of an expanding corps of forest police cannot keep migrant gatherers and hunters out of the Green Sea. In 1988 the government decided to ban all private prospecting and panning for gold. Whether these rules actually could be enforced was not at all certain.

Fires are inevitable. Until recent years they had been confined largely to the Lesser Hinggan Range, which had been chewed away at for more than a hundred years, particularly by the Japanese occupants in the fifteen years of Manchukuo and World War II. Between 1966 and 1981 nearly five million acres of forest, mostly in the Lesser Hinggan, was burned, and half of this was burned over again. Forests are like virgins; once they are violated, the likelihood of repetition increases.

There had been two bad fires in Manchuria, one in 1948, before the People's Republic was established. This destroyed about 400,000 acres. Another in 1956 burned a million acres in the Lesser Hinggan. But the Greater Hinggan remained little touched. Its record had been especially good in 1985 and 1986. The fire loss in 1986 was the smallest on record, only about 30,000 acres. Some Chinese officials felt such sterling results might cause the rangers to lose vigilance. The men on the beat took issue. They believed their safety efforts were paying off and that the task of preserving the vast Green Sea was now moving ahead successfully.

Long before May 6, 1987, China's forest administrators had introduced elementary fire-protection measures — building more watchtowers, instituting patrols, hiring wardens and professional fire fighters — to protect the jewel of their forest treasures, the Hinggan reserves. They knew that thousands of years of tree cutting, fire, and depredation had turned huge regions of China into waterless, treeless wastes. The whole of the northwest, Xinjiang, and the Gansu corridor had been lost except for irrigated patches of oasis. Of a landscape devoid of trees, residents said, "We have only one wind: it blows all year." Agriculture and even life were almost impossible on these nude oceans of yellow, brown, and red earth. The thought that the northeast might be headed for the same fate was dreadful to contemplate.

China's timber had been exploited so ruthlessly that the Black Dragon Forest now represented about one third of all the nation had left. What with the explosive needs of new economic development, China was cutting 30 percent more timber than Canada each year, and even this was not enough. China's southern forests were vanishing. The Forestry Ministry estimated that half the southern forests would be totally cut within ten years and that by the year 2000 most of these southern forests would be gone. True, there had been a dramatic "mass" planting of trees during the Great Proletarian Cultural Revolution. All over China millions of men, women, and children clambered up to ten-inch terraces on high mountainsides or labored in blazing deserts, planting billions of young saplings. But by 1988 only one third of the saplings had survived. The rest withered away from lack of care.

Inextricably linked to human ravaging of forests are the natural forces that advance the cycle of destruction. For centuries China's greatest robbers have been wind and water erosion, dust, floods, and silt. The Yellow River is yellow with the farmlands of North and Northwest China; not for nothing has it been called China's sorrow. More ecological damage has been inflicted on China by deforestation than was wrought by warlords in thousands of years — and it goes forward at a quickening pace.

Equally devastating is the specter of desertification. The interiors of continents generate severe temperature contrasts, and these, in turn, produce strong prevailing winds. The winds increase in force as they move across areas not protected by vegetative cover, grasslands, or forest. As forests are cut or burned they become increasingly exposed to wind, and this sets in motion desertification in areas of low annual rainfall.

This process has been in progress in China for thousands of years. Deserts have moved remorselessly eastward across Northwest China, across Mongolia, and now lap at the fringes of Manchuria. Day by day relentless winds extend the boundaries of the Gobi, the Ordos, the Junggar, the Qaidam, and other deserts, steadily bringing them nearer and nearer to the Manchurian redoubt.

And meanwhile, the danger of fire in the Black Dragon Forest rose steadily as the Chinese began more intense exploitation of the Hinggan resources. That handmaiden of logging, forest fire, could not be far behind. It is a law of the forest that the first fire is almost inevitably followed by a second, a third, a fourth. The carbon bed left by the first fire, the quick regeneration of trash timber, accumulation of forest debris, and the increased fire hazards caused by human influx multiply the dangers at roulette odds.

Total destruction of the Black Dragon Forest would cause incalculable damage, both to China and the rest of the world. First, China's balance of food production and population is already critically poised. The possibility of accelerated loss of agricultural lands and forest-lands — even now a serious problem in Manchuria, where one of the world's most severe continental climates has combined with deforestation to render vast areas unsuitable for farming — poses questions of survival. China's goal of entering the ranks of the world's moderately developed economies (Rumania, Spain) by the middle of the twenty-first century would be doomed. Further, great forests are not merely reservoirs of economic wealth; they are environmental generators of gigantic scale. What happened to Black Dragon would affect not only Manchuria, China, Mongolia, Korea, and Japan, but also world climatology. On a global level the prospective increase in aridity and wind force threatens the weather pattern that sweeps east from the North Asian rim across the Pacific and ultimately over the continental United States.

The rise of a new "weather furnace" in Manchuria could affect world climate in ways too complex for meteorological prediction. But in China the reappearance of the devastating Beijing dust storms was seen by popular opinion as a foretaste of what might be expected.

China was not alone in her concern. Specialists in many countries were eyeing the forest warily. International silviculturists, aware of the environmental changes flowing from the piecemeal destruction of the conifer belt that once extended from New England to the Pacific Northwest — more severe temperatures, massive soil erosion, lake and stream pollution, wind erosion, devastating river floods, recurrent drought — feared a duplication of this in East Asia. Extinction of the Black Dragon conifer sea, they felt, would constitute an act of global violence akin to nuclear war.

Thinking of this order led the Canadian government, after careful studies, to suggest to China that, should Beijing so desire, a small, pragmatic training program could be created to share Canada's advanced expertise in forest-fire prevention and fire-fighting techniques. No other country in the world has had so many fire problems nor developed more talents in coping with them. The program was tiddledywinks by international-aid standards — $4.7 million in Canadian funds and a handful of fire specialists. It was authorized in 1983, and by the summer of 1987 thirty-one Chinese foresters had come to Canada and twenty-six Canadians to China, mostly to Jiagedaqi, where they set up headquarters in the courtyard of the Forest Sea Hotel, in a neat-as-a-pin three-room Canadian prefab about as big as a couple of recreational vehicles. Beside the headquarters was a miniature prefab, a shed for their fire equipment. They brought in some of their newest wind blowers, which turn fires back on themselves, and lightweight swatters, which ease the rugged task of beating out a fire.

On May 6, 1987, Jack Minor, a compact, hard-muscled Canadian from Kenora, on the Minnesota-Ontario border, was occupying the prefab (nicknamed Jiapro) with his wife. Although the taciturn fire fighter would never use the word, like most of the Canadians he had come to worship the Black Dragon Forest. He had thought of little else since his first trip in 1985. He admired and respected his Chinese colleagues, particularly Commander Ge Xueling, who had spent time in Canada and whose offices were in a building a hundred feet from the prefab.

Minor admitted he was somewhat in awe of the forest. It was the greatest in the world if the Soviet portion was counted in. After the fire he allowed sadly that he had seen many, too many, burned forests — but never devastation like that of the Black Dragon fire.

Sitting in his squeaky-clean quarters on May 6, Minor followed his usual routine. He worked over a report to Ottawa while his wife went out shopping in the markets, a task she enjoyed. She liked the street life of Jiagedaqi, the children in their bright clothes and the mothers examining the fresh vegetables brought in from the country — mostly cabbage at this season. Minor listened to the BBC world news, as he did every evening. He and his wife ate supper in the little dining nook of the prefab. All was quiet. Usually some Chinese colleagues dropped by for a chat. No one came by that night, but Minor thought nothing of it.

The next day, May 7, he noticed signs that something unusual was afoot. There was much coming and going at the forest headquarters across the compound from the prefab. Toward evening one of the Chinese came by and told him a fire had broken out at the Gulian forest farm, but he said he didn't think it was too serious.

Not until May 8, when Minor found that most of the top officials had left for the forest, did he realize that the situation must be bad. Later, as he reconstructed events, he came to believe that his Chinese colleagues hadn't thought the fire was especially serious until the evening of the seventh or the morning of the eighth.

Jack Minor has fought so many forest fires in Canada he can't begin to remember them all. He thinks he has fought at least a thousand. Some of his friends believe the total may be twice that. He was an early smoke jumper, and he helped develop many modern techniques of fighting fires. He is accustomed to jumping by parachute from a low-flying patrol plane in the rear of a forest blaze, setting fire to grass or bush to burn out a secure base for himself and a team of jumpers, moving up to attack the blaze directly, setting backfires by burning areas ahead of the fire so that it will stutter to a halt in an already burned zone, moving in with blowers to blow the fire back on itself or calling in the remarkable scooper planes that the Canadians have designed. These aircraft, specially built with a belly scoop, swoop low over a lake, fill the belly with water, then fly to the fire, pouring water on the leading edges to halt or delay its progress.

There is nothing Jack Minor doesn't know about fighting fires. As he sat in his prefab, waiting for the Chinese to drop by, he couldn't help feel that he should be out fighting the fire. But he was never asked. Later

Minor rationalized his experience. The fire was such a disaster that the Chinese felt it was a matter of pride to handle it themselves. To have called on foreign experts, even ones whom they trusted, like Minor and the other Canadians, would have seemed an admission that they were still dependent on outside expertise. This was something they *had* to handle themselves, a matter of national pride, of national maturity, a sign that they were no longer incapable of taking care of their own emergencies. This was one of the things that Mao Zedong had taught them. Self-reliance, even if they could not do the job well. Independence. Pride of nationhood. As Mao preached, "China has stood up." To turn to foreign friends in an emergency would be a sign of weakness.

Minor's estimation was probably right, because when formal offers of assistance were made by foreign countries the Chinese did not rush to accept them. Only after ten days were some of them taken up. This was especially true in cases where protocol required that a formal Chinese request for assistance be made. The technicalities were fulfilled — but only after a wait, as if to downplay any sense of urgency or dependence. There may also have been a bureaucratic factor. To call for foreign help might be seen as an admission of bureaucratic weakness, improper planning, lack of foresight.* I think the Chinese may have been surprised that the United States did not rush forward with a major offer of technical assistance (even though it would

* Late in 1988 the Chinese formally changed this policy, permitting the acceptance of foreign aid in disasters without bureaucratic delay.

not have been quickly approved), but they were pleased by a more modest contribution, from "Paulo Solo." The party secretary of Tahe told me about "Solo," who he believed was an American writer, perhaps a poet. He didn't have his address, but he hoped I would convey the thanks of the fire victims. On a hunch from Helen Stephenson of the Authors League I called Paolo Soleri, the architect and environmentalist in Arizona. Soleri casts bells in porcelain or bronze. His foundation, Cosanti, sends $16 of each bell's $80 purchase price to a cause of the customer's choice. An American going to China in spring 1987 bought a bell and asked that the contribution go to China's fire victims.

When I drove down the gravel road toward the Gulian farm on September 15, 1987, the first hint I had that we were approaching the place where the Black Dragon fire started was the sight of the young policeman who, I had been told, was one of the first summoned to the scene. Now he stood beside the road ready to tell me what he had found after responding to the call from Gulian. Word of the fire reached Xilinji around 3:15 P.M. on May 6, and he was sent to investigate. After biking the eight miles in half an hour he found a fire burning over two hundred to three hundred acres. Several hundred men from the farm were fighting it, and they expected to contain it without too much trouble. Brush Cutter Wang was still on the scene, as was Li Yi, the section chief who had put him on the payroll. The policeman questioned both, as well as the Gulian supervisors and other members of the work team. Then he took Wang and Li Yi back to Xilinji and put them in jail. They were later transferred to Jiagedaqi, where they still languished when I visited the fire scene.

When the policeman left to take the men to jail, darkness had fallen and the fire was burning briskly, but the fire-fighting force had grown to more than a thousand men. Confidence was high that the fire would soon be under control.

IV

Yan Jinchun and the Second Battalion

AMONG THE FIRE FIGHTERS was the Second Battalion of Division 81158, commanded by a tall, broad-shouldered officer, Yan Jinchun, a no-nonsense army man. There are always a good many PLA units in the forest region because the Black Dragon River forms the border with the Soviet Union. Even with the border quiet, PLA units spend a good deal of time there on construction jobs. The tension and even shooting in the not distant past have not been forgotten.

Yan had been ordered up from Harbin with his battalion to build a five-mile timber road on the Gulian tract. He arrived April 27, 1987, stationing his five companies at intervals of about a mile along the route of the proposed road. He gave his men a few days to set up tents, organize their camps, get their gear in order, and learn the lay of the land. He put his own headquarters at the pithead of the Gulian coal mine, about eight miles from the Gulian forest farm. At 1:30 A.M. on the night of May 6–7 a jeep slewed to a stop outside his door. It was the motor chief of the Gulian farm, asking for help with the fire. Yan had no fire experience, but his men did possess axes, shovels, and picks. He loaded up his headquarters company immediately, and the others tailed along as soon as messengers gave them the orders to follow. On the way to the fire they broke off branches with which to beat out the flames.

About two miles from Gulian, Yan smelled the smoke and saw the flames. The fire was spreading along both sides of the road leading to Xilinji. By 3:00 A.M. his men took their places on the fire lines. County officers were directing the battle. Yan heard a lot of angry talk about Brush Cutter Wang. Had Wang still been there he probably would have been hurled into the fire. The glint in Yan's eye suggested to me that he would have joined gladly in the task.

Yan's job was to keep the fire from spreading along the road toward Xilinji. The battle went well. The smoke rose straight to the sky. There was no wind. Night is the best time to fight forest fires because the atmospheric pressure tends to be lower then. By 4:00 A.M. the spread of the fire had been halted. It had been contained within an area of about four square miles. At midmorning on May 7 no more smoke could be seen rising from the fire. The battle was won.

But no one was taking chances. Although no fire or smoke could be seen, hidden sparks might reignite the timber. Yan spaced his men at fifty-yard intervals along the road to watch for any upsurge and himself patrolled the perimeter. The fifteen hundred civilian workers maintained a similar vigil. If a little rain could be coaxed out of the clouds, the threat would be over.

Commander Ge Xueling, vice director of the Fire Control Center for the Greater Hinggan Forest, was thirty-nine years old when I met him in 1987. This tall, straight, handsome man was born in 1948, the year the People's Liberation Army took Manchuria. His birthplace was Fuyin, in the heart of the Green Sea, in the Lesser Hinggan Forest. His name means "study the forest." He has a brother called Study Wood. His sister is Study Mountains.

In a scarlet jacket, whipcord breeches, and a ranger's broad-brimmed Stetson, Commander Ge would look the very model of a Canadian Royal Mountie. He learned his English in a six-month crash course at the Beijing Language Training Center. Two visits to Canada have given him a detectable Canadian accent. He knows Sault Ste. Marie and Thunder Bay, and he loves trout fishing. "I'm very good at trout fishing," he brags. "I can beat my Canadian friends."

Commander Ge is a key man in the Chinese-Canadian forestry program. No man loves the forest more than he. He has named his thirteen-year-old daughter Haijing, which means "crystal in the sea," or "dew," and carries the poetic fragrance of both the forest and the sea. His eleven-year-old son is called Haifeng, which suggests a mountain peak surrounded by a sea of forest or, alternately, huge waves of the sea. Commander Ge's father was a woodworker, spending his life in the forest. Clearly, the commander expects his children to carry on the family's dedication to the Hinggan forests. They are keepers of the faith.

Commander Ge had watched the advent of spring 1987 with apprehension. His eighteen years in the Forest Service had taught him how to sense danger. His practical experience was backed up with study at the Northeast Forest University, which he entered after graduation from high school in 1964. As vice director of the Fire Control Center, Ge earned 170 yuan, about $125, a month. This was in the medium range for civil servants. Before concentrating on fire control, Ge had served in the forest police. He and his family lived in a pleasant four-room apartment close by his office across the courtyard from the Forest Sea Hotel. He was the top-level antifire engineer in the forest. No one in China knew the forest as did he. He was ever on the go, inspecting areas of his responsibility. In spring and autumn he patrolled by helicopter. In summer and winter — seasons of less danger — he roamed the territory by jeep, always insisting on seeing with his own eyes, testing the dryness of the forest floor with his own hands.

There had been almost no rain in the summer of 1986, and the winter was barren of snow. Usually there is a foot or more of snow cover in the winter, depending on altitude, and a big blizzard snugs down the forest in late March or early April. The melt and runoff saturate the woods and carry them through the peak fire period of April and May. Summer rains dampen the forest for the autumn peril in September and October.

Timbering is not a private industry in China, as it was in Minnesota. There are no timber kings like the

Peaveys or Weyerhaeusers. Nor are there any robber barons, who in Minnesota clear-cut half a state without bothering to own too many of the trees that rode down the Mississippi to the great sawmills of Minneapolis. But the forest farms are run for profit. They are money-making entities, the managers pressed by the state to boost output and boost revenues. The results are not too different from those of the robber barons. The Chinese said they did not engage in clear-cutting, that is, cutting all the trees in sight like an old-time barber with his clippers. But their hand was often heavy. Whatever the philosophy of the forest farms, they were lifting production and lifting it again. Most of the cutting was, of course, carried out in winter, and the cut in the winter of 1986–87 had been the highest ever. The farms were off to a flying start. Or so it seemed.

This spring, however, Commander Ge was worried. High winds often strike the Black Dragon area in spring, flowing east from the denuded land and deserts of the west. The forests were dry. There had been no big spring snowfall. Temperatures were high. The ground was warm and hard.

Because of the heavy demand for lumber the forest farms had concentrated for two or three years on increasing their output. Not only were timbering operations being stepped up, but logging debris — very combustible — was piling up in the woods as the farms neglected cleanup operations in order to boost the output of logs. This was another worry for Commander Ge. There was a buildup of very dry vegetable materials and combustibles. In places it was two and three feet deep on the forest floor. When the snow cover was normal it was hard even to light a campfire in May. Now Ge feared that any cigarette stub might set off a conflagration. "We had been concerned since autumn 1986," he said. "We were well aware of the dangerous conditions which existed. This forest is the biggest in the world and its protection was my responsibility."

They did what they could. They alerted the forest farm managements; they sent in more rangers and forest police and held helicopters in reserve. The Greater Hinggan Forest presented difficulties for helicopter observation because of its density, but this density provided some protection against fires. The Lesser Hinggan, much more open because of its mixture of deciduous trees, bare areas left by previous fire damage, and patchy grassland, was far more suitable to helicopter observation.

There had been seven small fires in the Greater Hinggan in April, a normal number. The few fires in the forest extension in Inner Mongolia gave little cause for fear.

Although Chinese satellites constantly monitor the Soviet side of the Black Dragon (and all of Siberia, for that matter), the Forestry Ministry does not receive their daily output on a routine basis. It requests photographs periodically. But, tragically, extremely accurate information about the start and spread of the fires was available yet, at least in the initial phases, was not made use of by the Forest Service. The data that could have made a difference were the observations of the Chinese Meteorological Service based on the U.S. Tiros polar-orbiting weather satellites. Two satellites are employed in the U.S. system, providing continuous observations within a six-hour period. The U.S. weather satellite signals are open to international use and have been employed by China for a number of years. The satellites are able to detect high-temperature targets (fires) in areas as small as an acre and can observe the fire plumes and identify the vegetation feeding the fire. The satellite transmissions are constantly received by the Chinese weather service and processed into images using computerized digital image processing, which provides pictures of surface fires and remaining burning areas. The process takes a little time but is fast enough for fire detection and fire-fighting purposes.

Chinese meteorologists were fully aware of the high hazard conditions that prevailed in the Heilongjiang Forest area and actually recorded the start of the fires as early as 3:42 P.M. (Beijing summer time) May 6. At that time three fires were shown by the satellite imaging: one at the Hu Wan forest farm, near Xilinji; one at Pangu, in Tahe County; and a third at the Yixi Forest, in Almu County. The Yixi fire did not develop. At 9 A.M. May 7 the Gulian fire turned up on the imaging.

The satellite images revealed the extraordinary speed of development of the fires, *averaging* up to 15 miles an hour, as well as their enormous spread — the Hu Wan fire developed a 150-mile front, while the front at Gulian was greater than 100 miles with smoke plumes as long as 425 miles and 60 or 70 miles wide. Based on this data, the Xilinji weather bureau had issued a class 5 (highest danger) fire alert on May 7.

But little, if any, of this data was provided to the fire

fighters in the Black Dragon Forest before the evening of May 7, probably because of reasons of economy and, possibly, bureaucracy. In fact, the existence of this data was never mentioned to me in the forest area nor by forestry officials in Beijing. It was finally provided in the United States by the American meteorological specialist Associate Professor Alan Robock of the University of Maryland.

The fires on the Soviet side of the Black Dragon started, as later inspection revealed, about fifteen days ahead of the Chinese fires. However, initially they were not visible from the Chinese side of the river. Their extent became known to Commander Ge and his associates only when they requested prints after the outbreak at Gulian. Ge estimated that the largest Soviet fire covered at least 32,000 square miles. China's burned-over span covered some 6,400 square miles. By contrast Canada's Red Lake fire, which occurred about the same time, covered only 700 square miles. Many Chinese believed that some climatic factor, not understood, caused a simultaneous breakout of fires around the world in Canada, the United States, China, and the Soviet Union, all in the 50-degree-latitude range. In 1988 the Yellowstone National Park fire, in the United States, affected an area about half the size of that ravaged by the Chinese fire. However, U.S. park officials estimated that actual burned acreage in the Yellowstone forest amounted to only a very small percentage of the affected region.

Commander Ge pointed out a bit wryly that the Soviet fire burned for forty-five days and the Chinese for only thirty-two days. The Russians, he said, often make little attempt to fight fires in the forests east of Lake Baikal because they do not intend to launch timber operations there for another hundred years, by which time, they hope, the forest will have regenerated. The Russian forest is at least ten times larger than the Chinese. In the spring of 1987 the only active Soviet fire intervention of which the Chinese were aware occurred when fires approached towns and cities. The Soviet airport at Chita, however, was closed repeatedly, they said, because of heavy smoke.

In fact, despite Chinese fears, there was no direct connection between the Soviet and Chinese fires. Soviet sparks did not ignite Chinese forests, nor did Chinese fires cause destruction of Soviet land. The fires on either side of the Black Dragon River were products of identical conditions: dry forests, high winds.

Commander Ge considered that it would be most helpful if the fire-fighting collaboration of the 1950s could be restored. In those days the Russians had permitted the Chinese to cross the frontier to get easier access to remote fires. The two countries established a joint fire station at Qiqihar, but the fire-control protocol had been a dead letter since 1960. According to Soviet ambassador Oleg Troyanovsky, in Beijing, the Chinese informally approached Russia at the height of the Black Dragon fire. They asked whether the Soviets would permit Chinese fire-fighting helicopters to fly over the Soviet side of the Black Dragon if necessary to combat the fire. Troyanovsky said that permission had been given and that Moscow had offered additional helicop-

The Heilongjiang, or Black Dragon, River (known in the west as the Amur) separates China and the Soviet Union along the area of the Black Dragon fire. Here is a view of the stream at Mohe, looking toward the Soviet side.

Chinese troops coming up to the burning Black Dragon Forest, seeking to hold a road line against the spread of the fire.

The author and a Chinese soldier looking toward the desolate spot near the Gulian forest farm where the Black Dragon fire broke out.

Ruins of the workshop of Li Songlin. He lost two shops in Xilinji worth 100,000 yuan (about $30,000).

Night battle against the Black Dragon Forest fire.

Burning wooden houses at Xilinji.

Fire victims being evacuated by army truck.

Black Beard, hero of the Black Dragon fire. As a deputy division commander of the Chinese army he led the fight against the fire in the eastern sector of the forest. Violating army rules, he let his beard grow for twenty-five days during the day-and-night struggle against the flames, finally shaving when the danger was past.

ters if the Chinese needed them (the Chinese fire-fighting helicopters are Russian-made). The Chinese did not take up the offer. Chinese forestry officials insisted they had never heard of it.

Commander Ge's high cheekbones give his profile a faint resemblance to that of the American Indian who used to adorn the U.S. one-cent piece. Now, as he spoke with me several months after the fire, it took on a somber aspect.

"Yes," he said, "we were aware of the possibility of a great fire and that it would be beyond the possibility of our control."

The danger of high wind never left his mind. "With a high wind you can't halt a fire," he said. "So far as I know there is no capability in the United States, Canada, or the Soviet Union that can halt such a fire."

On May 6, the day Brush Cutter Wang spilled some gasoline, Commander Ge, making his incessant rounds, was at Tahe, about eighty miles north of his Jiagedaqi headquarters. A report he received during the evening said that a fire had broken out at Gulian. It did not suggest that bringing the fire under control was beyond the ability of the competent local foresters.

Ge went to bed that night as uneasy as he had been for weeks. First thing in the morning he would check Gulian and make certain that nothing had gotten out of hand.

On the morning of May 7 the Gulian fire seemed under control to Commander Yan Jinchun. Nevertheless, he stayed on watch with his Second Battalion. The forest was so dry that no one could be sure the fire would not break out again.

About 3:30 that afternoon Yan was with his men, ten miles south of Xilinji, when he noticed the wind begin to rise. For many hours the air had been almost still. Now the aspens were rustling under gusts from the northwest. Hardly had he felt the wind rise than he saw a wisp of smoke rising some distance down the fire line. The wind blew stronger, and by 4:00 P.M. the wisp had become a pillar of black smoke towering hundreds of feet in the air. It reminded Yan of the mushroom cloud of the atom bomb.

Yan alerted his men and had them start work on a firebreak, but for the most part they could only watch and wait. The smoke was not rising from their sector.

"I had lots of experience with disasters, even earthquakes, but I had never seen anything like this," he said.

Just about 4:00 P.M. the county authorities instructed him to move his troops back to a new defense line about four miles west of Xilinji. He bundled his men into six trucks and rumbled down the gravel road. He could see that the fire was following them, not more than six hundred feet behind. He called the county leadership on his walkie-talkie. They told him to hurry his men to the county ammunitions dump, on the northern outskirts of town. The explosives stored there were used by the militia, to which almost all young men and women belonged. His order was to protect the depot from the fire at all costs.

The depot was a brick structure, half belowground,

half above. Yan's men dug a firebreak fifty feet wide and two hundred yards long. It took an hour. By then the fire was almost on them, a blanket of flame a hundred feet high propelled by a wind of force 6 or 7, that is, 25 to 38 miles an hour. (This scale is the standard Beaufort wind measurement, internationally used in ocean navigation and in some countries for land winds.)

"The moment the firebreak was finished," Commander Yan said, "we jumped into our trucks and hurried off. We didn't want to be around if the arms dump blew up."

It didn't. The flames whooshed over the top of the depot and charged on to the city, less than a mile away. By now, some witnesses said, the wind was hurling fireballs the size of basketballs through the air. Anything they touched burst into flames.

Xilinji was a city of twenty-two thousand, totally devoted to lumber. Forest fires were nothing new. Several times a year all the men were mobilized to beat back fires in the hills and mountains. It was a city of wood — wooden houses, wooden barracks, wooden offices, wooden warehouses. Near its center stood a great lumber stock of 100,000 cubic yards. It was soon blazing. Yan brought his trucks to the end of the highway and paused a moment before entering the city. He could not see through the dense smoke. He did not know whether his men and he would get out alive. He was drenched with sweat as he pondered his decision. Finally he plunged in, determined to rescue as many people as he could. But that was difficult. His trucks became separated almost immediately. It was a scene of chaos. Some buses and trucks were carrying people out of the city. They blindly crunched over mountains of bicycles discarded by people fleeing for their lives. Yan got out of his truck and led it by hand through the murk. For some reason he could see the backs of heads better than faces. Everything was black.

There seemed to be three levels of smoke. From the ground to the knees it was dark and full of pitch. There was a yellow, resinous level above that. Head high, the smoke was whitish and the air hot as an oven. A political instructor in Yan's outfit, a man weighing more than two hundred pounds, jumped from his truck and felt the wind take his legs out from under him and drop him on the ground. He could hardly get up.

I asked Yan whether he was frightened. He looked at me as though I were an idiot. "Of course I was frightened," he said. "There was fire everywhere. I thought I would die. I had that thought from the beginning. I kept thinking it to the end."

He paused, his mind running back over the experience.

"I thought that whatever happened I should rescue people," he said. "Then we would all die together. If I died I wanted to die with them. Hope was very thin."

Fire destroyed one of Yan's trucks, damaged two others. His corps led more than two hundred women and children out of the city and one or two elderly men. The rest of the men were all fighting the fire. Sometimes the smoke was so thick people couldn't breathe. They slithered on the ground like a company of snakes. His men formed them into hollow squares with a soldier ahead and one behind to help any strag-

glers. Yan lost no men, but forty-one, including himself, were burned, mostly on the hands and face.

"Yes," he pondered, "it was as bad as a battle. Maybe
worse."

His battalion, the first to enter the struggle against the
fire, was designated a Hero Battalion by Deng Xiaoping. The honor had not been bestowed since the Korean War.

The wind did not remain constant. When Commander Yan and his men pulled out of Xilinji at 11:30 P.M.
they were ordered back to Gulian. Fire was again bearing down on the forest farm, this time from neighboring Hu Wan farm, which had been burned out
despite the efforts of the Seventh Heavy Artillery Regiment stationed at nearby Luoguhe.* For thirty-two
days the Second Battalion would fight fire after fire
until the last was out. Not until June 6 did it return to
normal duties.

---

*Satellite photos examined later indicated that the Hu Wan fire started well
before the Gulian fire, but the location was so remote that the Xilinji authorities apparently were unaware of the blaze.

V

Political Director Wang Aiwu

IN A STATE OF CHAOS, each man or woman sees only a fragment of the whole. So it was for the Black Dragon kingdom in the time of the fire. The people in one part of Xilinji did not know what was happening in another. The people in Tuqing, the next town to the east, did not know what was going on in Xilinji. Back at Tahe, at his frontline headquarters, Commander Ge Xueling did not know what was happening at Xilinji, at Tuqing, or even at Pangu and Walagan, which were just to his west on the railroad spur, only forty and twenty miles away.

Commander Ge had come to Tahe because his communications to the forest stations were as good at this secondary headquarters as at the Fire Control Center in Jiagedaqi and because here he was strategically located at the eastern end of the railroad spur. He could quickly reach the forest areas to the west by rail or by his standby helicopter.

The news during the morning and early afternoon of May 7 was worrisome but not alarming. The fire at

Gulian had been brought under control. However, the Gulian fire was not the only one on Commander Ge's field map. Late in the afternoon of May 6, at 5:40 P.M., a fire had been reported at one of the Pangu forest farms, roughly halfway between Xilinji and Tahe. The Pangu headquarters told Commander Ge that they were not alarmed, even though the fire had spread over several hundred acres. By the morning of May 7 two thousand men were on the fire lines. Although the fire had spread both to the east and to the west, the fighters felt they were getting the upper hand.

Ge spent the day checking and rechecking the forest. He patiently phoned one forest farm after another, he checked the weather stations by phone and wireless, he called the forest bureaus and the military commands. He was like the chief of staff at battle headquarters. He entered every scrap of information on his situation map, every wind shift, every assignment of fire fighters, every indication of fires dying down or spreading out. He shifted ranger teams from one locality to another as danger ebbed and flowed. He knew that a fire that had broken out at Hu Wan farm, to the north of Gulian, was still burning. There seemed to be one or two other small fires. It was not the size of the fires that worried Ge; it was the number of them and the quickness with which they had sprung up. He was contending not just with the error of an untrained brush cutter. He faced a condition in which error could become remarkably dangerous in a small space of time.

As the afternoon of May 7 drew to a close, the event over which Commander Ge had been worrying for nearly eighteen months began to happen, and when it began it moved at the speed of the wind roaring in from the northwest — a speed that went from force 6 or 7 to force 9 and above in a matter of minutes. The air that had been still as death suddenly began to blow at about 25 or 35 miles an hour and rose swiftly to gust at roughly 50 miles an hour and above.

Ge was at the eastern end of the threatened segment of the forest. As the wind moved from west to east, the fire snapped communications as if they were beads on a chain, cutting telephone and telegraph lines. Ge and the whole forest apparatus effectively were blinded.

The first point to be lost was Xilinji, the western anchor. It went out at 7:10 P.M. Next was Tuqing, forty miles east of Xilinji. It was lost at 8:00 P.M. Amur, fifteen miles farther east, hung on until 10:10 P.M. By that time Commander Ge knew that the dimensions of the crisis were as broad as the forest.

The town of Xilinji is shaped like a slightly elongated box. Because of Xilinji's location along the Tang Ta River, a tributary of the Emur, its streets run not north-south and east-west but northwest-southeast and northeast-southwest. The Tang Ta River lies north and east on the outskirts of the city, and a bridge connects the city with the gravel road to the Black Dragon River and Mohe, about fifty miles to the northeast. The east-west railroad spur runs along the western edge of the city and then turns southwest to the Gulian forest farm.

To the south of the city there is a low range of hills from which a panoramic view of the town can be had. There are also hills along the northwestern fringe of town, and it was from these hills that the fire descended

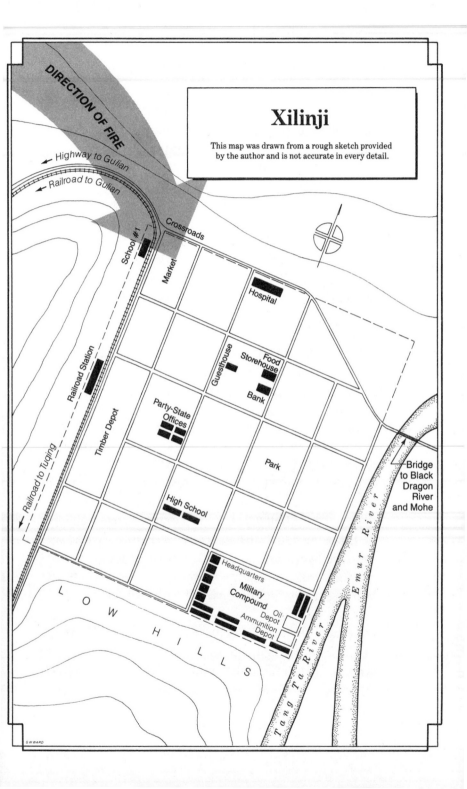

on Xilinji. The principal buildings — the railroad station, post office, School Number 1 (a high school), government and party offices, guesthouse, hospital, and banks — were located in the northern half of the city. The school was in the northwest at a crossroads facing a wide, open square where the free market in meat, vegetables, clothing, and secondhand goods had been located since Deng Xiaoping's relaxation of private trade and commerce. Midway along the western flank of the city stood the railroad station and post office. Close to the railroad before the fire stood the principal timber depot with tens of thousands of logs and stored timber awaiting shipment. On the southeastern outskirts of the town, not far from the Tang Ta River, sprawled the Ninth Regiment military compound.

The rest of town was given over to small shops and housing, some private, some barracks, almost all one-story wooden structures. Near the center of town was a pleasant park of virgin conifers, uncut and left as a monument to the forest that once grew on the spot where the town was founded in 1974.

When I saw Xilinji this geography was difficult to reconstruct. The entire city had been destroyed by the fire except for half a dozen brick and concrete buildings of three or four stories. These structures were surrounded by devastation. Intensive construction was going forward. Thousands of carpenters labored to get housing up before the onset of early winter.

On May 6 Political Director Wang Aiwu was in charge of the Ninth Regiment of the PLA because his two seniors, the commander and the deputy commander, were in Harbin undergoing medical treatment. Most of the troops were on duty along the border.

On the morning of May 7 Director Wang had been briefed on Gulian. The fire was under control, but a shortage of food for the fire fighters had developed. The director drew supplies from the regimental stocks and had them on their way in two hours.

The Ninth Regiment compound was a spacious area in southeastern Xilinji, comprising a large courtyard bigger than a parade ground, commodious barracks, an excellent headquarters building, four other good-sized buildings, and big ammunition and oil depots (not the county ammo depot saved by the timely action of Commander Yan Jinchun).

At 6:00 P.M. on May 7 Director Wang saw from his courtyard that the wind was rising fast and the town was becoming shrouded in smoke. He estimated the wind at just short of 50 miles an hour.

"I witnessed this," the director said, a little dramatically. "Within thirty or forty minutes the situation had become terrifying. The fire was beyond control. The need was to save the people. The fire might be compared to a typhoon, the waves were coming at express speed. The situation was one of terror and danger. It was unlike anything I had seen."

Amid all this he was, he said, tremendously impressed with the calm and heroism of the county leaders and forest men. They kept working quietly on a firebreak with the flames only a block distant. But they could not stop the fire.

He took a detachment of a hundred men into town and led them to the western highway. The streets were almost impassable, and he decided to go back to protect his headquarters and the ammo and oil depots, to mobilize his men, and to turn the compound into a refugee center. By the direction of the wind Wang knew the compound would be in the fire's path. He hoped its great expanse of open ground would save it from destruction. His men had to fight their way through the crowds streaming from the city. Back at the compound he found his men scattered throughout the area, and he had trouble rounding them up. Ordinarily he summoned them with a bugle call. But this was now impossible — the call was recorded on tape, and the electricity was out.

He had one concern. If his ammunition and petrol dumps blew up, the blast would equal a small atom bomb, enough to wipe out headquarters and the city.

Wang decided to take a chance. He ordered the gates opened. People swarmed in. "They didn't know what they were doing," he said. One woman was carrying her baby upside down. The child's face was blanched. He put the child right side up. Women clutched at his hands. He told them to stop running, find a place on the ground, and sit down. A lady in her seventies cried: "What do I do now?" He said: "Calm down. Go sit on that bench and keep your mouth open." An hour later he came by. She was still sitting there, her mouth open. He told her she could close it now.

Director Wang had taken a calculated gamble when he opened the compound gates. The fire had come down from the northwestern hills and was cutting a broad swath through the town from northwest to

southeast. The compound lay on the far eastern outskirts of town, but as the wind brought the flames into
town they touched off the wooden buildings, broaden-
ing the path of fire and moving it closer and closer to
the big compound.

Wang still had a line open to the military command
of the Black Dragon area. He took the precaution of
asking for instructions. The answer came back: give
priority to protecting the ammunition and oil depots.
Defend them against destruction at all costs.

Soon the fire began to threaten both refugees and
depots. A fireball from the northwestern hills rocketed
into the third floor of the headquarters building, and
the floor exploded in flames. Sparks and fiery debris
catapulted into the camphor trees that shaded the compound.

Within half an hour of Wang's decision to let the
people into the compound, it became clear that they
could be trapped in a whirlwind of flame. The ammunition dump was located fifteen hundred feet away at the
southwestern edge of the big compound. Embers
lodged in a pile of creosoted logs beside the ammunition dump, a brick and concrete vault fitted with an
iron door and packed with tons of shells, mines,
grenades, fuses, and bullets. The fire fighters threw
sand on the logs. It didn't help much.

Somehow wind whipped open the iron door beside
the blazing logs. Three soldiers ran to close it. Two were
driven back by the pitch-laden smoke. The third
poured water over his cotton padded jacket and made
his way to the clanging door. He managed to slam it

closed at the cost of burned hands and face. He was one of thirty-two men in the regiment to be decorated for bravery.

Fire moved closer and closer to the five thousand refugees assembled on the parade grounds. When it began to leap from one camphor tree to another, Director Wang sent in a team of soldiers with axes. They cut the trees, one by one, those burning, those yet unburned. When the brick building that housed headquarters began to burn, Wang ordered soldiers to wet blankets and hang them over the windows of the upper stories to prevent sparks and embers from spreading the flames from floor to floor. The wind whipped the blankets from the hands of the men. Some soldiers were almost hurled to the ground.

Hardly had the danger to the ammo depot been averted when the asphalt roof of the oil-storage vault, at the southeast corner of the compound, caught fire. Troops dampened their cotton comforters and used them to douse the blaze. Then they draped more wet comforters over the asphalt to catch the rain of sparks carried by the wind.

Other soldiers jumped into water reservoirs, soaking their jackets, then rolled over and over in the flaming grass to keep fire out of the parade quadrangle, where the refugees were clustered. Later the men got a "Rolling Over the Fire" medal, created specially for the occasion.

As fire surrounded the parade grounds, sparks flying overhead, flames shooting from buildings, smoke enshrouding the scene, pandemonium broke out. Women had brought all of their possessions they could carry on their backs — TV sets, radios, bedding, pots and pans, cotton sacks of valuables. Now they feared they would lose everything, including their lives. The women shouted. Babies howled.

Wang consulted the city authorities. He had real fear that the flames — hardly a hundred yards away — might break through. The ammunition might blow up or the gasoline catch fire.

It was decided to truck the people to safer spots. It was now close to 9:00 P.M. The fire had passed over the river. Many refugees were taken to the water's edge. Others were carried by a roundabout route to the high-way crossroads beside School Number 1, which had become the main assembly point for burned-out families.

When all the refugees had been removed, Wang began to assess the results. He and his men had saved the lives of more than five thousand people. Not one of those he had taken in had been injured. Nor had any of his men lost their lives. True, while they were caring for the refugees, their own barracks and houses in the compound had burned. They had lost all they had: furniture, color TV sets, electric refrigerators, bedding, clothing. But no one lost a wife or child. No one in the command had been seriously injured. The worst damage was scorched skins and hands, including those of Director Wang.

Sun Shangchun is a strong man, with a jutting jaw, a take-charge manner, and a different sense of the Black Dragon fire. He drives the bus every Monday, Wednesday, Friday, and Sunday from Mohe to Xilinji and back, a round trip of about a hundred miles through the forest. He starts each morning from Mohe.

Sun Shangchun leads a comfortable life. On the day I visited, his sunny house, one side all windows facing south, was almost a greenhouse, filled with plants and flowers. The new linoleum on the floor, in a geometric white-on-brown pattern, was better than any you could find in a Beijing department store. He displayed some family photos in big colored enlargements and, under glass, pictures of pretty girls cut out from Chinese magazines. Bric-a-brac filled a glass cabinet.

Sun's wife, a hardy-looking lady in green sweater and gray woolen trousers, was cooking lunch on a wood-fired iron stove. It smelled good. This family had it made. Sun was paid 220 yuan a month for driving the bus, his wife 145 for taking tickets, and his daughter 110 for working in the dispatcher's office — 475 yuan, nearly $200, take-home pay, comfortably rich by Chinese standards. There were glistening ropes of gold and silver tinsel festooning the chandelier, a leftover from New Year's celebrations.

Sun got out his trip book and checked the days of the big fire. No problems. He drove back and forth every day. The fire didn't bother him. He went to Xilinji the morning of May 6 and back in the evening. He went again and back on May 7. No problem. He brought four homeless people back to Mohe on the eighth. From then on he drove every day. Never even saw the fire. Ran into some choking smoke. He brought, his trip book indicated, about a thousand people back and forth in that time.

"No," he observed, tucking away the trip book, "it wasn't bad. Not bad at all."

Yes, some of his friends had trouble. One man's daughter was reduced to ashes, and a friend lost a son and daughter-in-law. The two were young people. They lacked experience. They were running along the highway. The fire was already on one side, and they tried to hide in the brush on the other side. They were choked to death by smoke. The party had shown his friend great consideration.

Sun and his friends had noted some curiosities about the fire. Many people were burned only on one side of the face. Often the fire had come up along one side of a road as those people raced away, trying to escape. A private truck, an old PLA Liberation model, was carrying a load of people out of the city. At the southeastern hills it ran off the road and into a tree. Those people who jumped to the right escaped. Those who jumped to the left were badly burned; one died. One of the lucky passengers in the truck was an older man, a private trader, a dealer in fruit and vegetables; he was uninjured. He had hoped to rent the truck and make 10,000 yuan, nearly $4,000, bringing food into the stricken city.

Bus Driver Sun is fond of life in Mohe. He grows eggplant, tomatoes, peppers, leeks, cabbage, potatoes, radishes. He raises chickens, the small, succulent Chinese kind. The fish from the Black Dragon River are plentiful. A bit of fish food at the open neck of the seine lures a cloud of little fish that look like small perch or big minnows. They are very tasty fried in peanut oil and a light batter. And, of course, there are what they call cold water fish, *xilim*, a kind of trout. The fishing in the Black Dragon is quite good now. The Soviet river patrols have quit harassing the Chinese so long as they stay close to the Chinese shore.

No, all things considered, Driver Sun feels there is much to be thankful for. He was lucky the fire didn't touch him. Of course there was a lot of smoke, thick smoke that made you cough, but after a couple of weeks it all went away.

VI

The Mayor of Xilinji

IN ADDITION to the Ninth Regiment facilities there are four other brick and concrete buildings in Xilinji — the party-government headquarters, the hospital, the school, and the guesthouse, where I was staying and conducting interviews. I had been told that the guesthouse had burned down and that I might have to live in a tent. Not at all. I was given a two-room suite. Sun poured in the windows, warm and cozy; there were a western toilet, newly painted red floor, green Chinese carpet, pink toilet paper, plenty of hot water, bowls of apples, Chinese pears, and a plate of bananas (from Colombia). The food was the best I had in the fire area. It was here that I met with the former mayor of Xilinji, Mrs. Wang Zhaowin.

I first heard of Mrs. Wang the day after I arrived in Xilinji. Guan Lianzeng, a county official, a bit on the excitable side, was telling me how the fire had descended on Xilinji. The wind came in from the west, he said, very strong, about force 9 (50 miles an hour), with flames rising more than a hundred feet in the air.

In forty minutes — that is, a bit after 7:00 P.M. — the city was engulfed in a sea of fire. The wind picked up the dust and blew it at your face. It stung like gravel.

At this point, he said, Mrs. Wang got into her jeep and went to the streets to warn the people to take shelter on the northwest side of town, already burned over in the first few minutes of the fire's attack. The mayor rode through town using a bullhorn to order citizens to come to the foot of the western hills, to the crossroads on the main highway beside School Number 1 and the free market. "She didn't ask them," he said. "She ordered them."

I later found that he had mixed up some details. Mrs. Wang did not go in the jeep herself. She sent a deputy to read her order. But she had been the hero of the fire, clear-headed, decisive, compassionate. This impression was deepened by the Ninth Regiment's political director, Wang Aiwu. She was, he said, a brave woman. She did everything a human being could do to halt the fire and save the city and its people. (Incidentally, none of the Wangs in this narrative were related. There are only a hundred family names in China, and Wang is more common than Smith is in the United States.)

I said I must talk to Mrs. Wang. There seemed to be a little embarrassment. She no longer was mayor. But I insisted, and on the morning of September 16 I found myself in the presence of a small, intense woman, with haunting eyes, plain gray tunic, black trousers (standard cadre dress), white blouse, just a glimpse under her man-cut jacket of a cardigan embroidered with rose and green flowers. She wore her hair in a rice bowl cut, a little tousled by the wind, a fringe of bangs, artificial mother-of-pearl buttons on her jacket. Her shoes were good black leather with white bobby socks. No jewelry but a silvery metal watch on her wrist. Businesslike.

She had graceful, long fingers, nails well tended. If she was a little tense, well, meeting an American reporter in this out-of-the-way corner after the trauma of the fire was not exactly your everyday experience. But there were only simplicity and candor when she began to tell what had happened, what she had seen, what she had done. I sat beside her and she looked straight ahead, fixing her eyes on Mrs. Wu Jun, a translator. They were of an age, both Red Guards in the Cultural Revolution; they understood each other. I noticed that the local officials who usually filled the room had absented themselves. The photographer took one picture, then left.

On May 6, 1987, Wang Zhaowin was the only woman of high rank in the five counties of the forest area. She had been sent to the Black Dragon country in 1967 when Mao Zedong, alarmed at the chaos created by his young Red Guards, began to ship them to the remote countryside to be "reeducated" by the peasants. Mrs. Wang was sixteen when she arrived in the rough borderland. By 1987 ninety-nine percent of the Red Guards had long since slipped back to the cities and their families, hating life so distant from Beijing and Shanghai, hating the forest, hating almost everything, themselves included, disillusioned by the fall from attending rallies with Chairman Mao in Tiananmen Square to tending pigsties and doing other menial chores in the countryside.

Not Wang Zhaowin. She had stayed. She had come to love the Green Sea, the silent world of needle-clad trees. She worked in the lumber camps, lived in barracks, went cold and hungry. Her hands grew red and callused, her back strong, her muscles firm, and her dark eyes stayed clear.

On the afternoon of May 6 Mrs. Wang was one of the first to hurry to Gulian to direct the fight against the fire. She had worked for twenty years in the forest. She knew how dry and dangerous it now was, and she knew the terrible wind, the *burya,* as the Siberians called it, that roared east from Lake Baikal.

Mrs. Wang spent most of the night at Gulian. By morning the fight was going well. With twelve hundred forest workers and the PLA's Second Battalion on the job the fire could be, should be, put out, if — the "if" was the wind. So far the air was quiet.

In the morning Mrs. Wang went back to the Ninth Regiment compound and told the acting commander, Wang Aiwu, that Gulian looked to be in pretty good shape but that she did not have enough food to feed the fire fighters. Could he help? He said he could.

Mrs. Wang was the county secretary of the party. Her responsibilities were comparable to those of an American mayor or county executive. Town and timber were her concerns. She continued to worry about Gulian. Another fire had broken out nearby, at the Hu Wan Forest, and she feared the two might join. At midafternoon of May 7 she went back to Gulian in her jeep to

take another look. She was there when the wind began
to rise. As the wind reignited the fire and whipped it
up, her driver raced her back into Xilinji ahead of the
flames. Already her task was clear: to save the town
and her people.

When Mrs. Wang began to talk, the room in which
we sat slipped away. I no longer saw the three wait-
resses in their electric-blue jackets and trousers, their
red sweaters, carrying tea bags and thermoses of boiling
water; the table with its tea mugs and ashtrays vanished, and I found myself in Xilinji on the night of May
7, the air hot as a dragon's breath, sky as black as pitch,
wind whirling up flaming tree branches and fireballs
coming in like cannon shot, one landing on an upper
floor of the PLA building, another hitting the Youth
Shop, a private enterprise. That was the end of the
Youth Shop.

The wind, Mrs. Wang calculated, was force 8 —
about 40 miles an hour — and the fire raged 150 feet in
the air. At first she had thought she might form a defense line in the center of the city, let the west side
burn, and save the east. This was nonsense. Dante's
inferno could not be smothered.

The important thing was the people. They were
terrified. They ran in circles. Some lugged electric refrigerators, TV sets, and sewing machines through the
dark turmoil, then dropped them and fled as a lick of
flame singed them.

Mrs. Wang issued orders, flat, arbitrary, military. She
did not get into her jeep. It had no loudspeaker. Her
deputy staggered in from Gulian, and she handed him
her proclamation and sent him out in the hospital am-

bulance, the only vehicle with a loudspeaker, to read it to the people. He read the orders in her name: "Forget your house. Forget your property. Save your life." She spoke simply, directly, as if to children. She knew people's minds were off the hook, distracted. There was no time for discussion. It was a time for orders.

As I listened she spoke steadily; she was composed, logical. Occasionally she used a slender finger to emphasize a point, leaning forward slightly, talking, talking, talking. She knew what she was doing that night. She had not lived and worked in the forest for twenty years for nothing. She knew fire. She knew the forest, knew the wind. She knew nature's tricks and dangers. It was a fight for life. No time to think. You either knew what to do or you perished. The safest place in a forest fire was the place the fire had just passed, the burned-over area behind the tail of the dragon. The most dangerous place was ahead of the fire, the fire leaping at your heels.

Her orders boomed from the ambulance speaker: "Go to the west. Go to the crossroads by School Number 1. Go to the open square." It was big enough. No claw of the dragon could reach the people there. The voice boomed again and again. But many still ran for the river bordering the eastern part of town. They huddled on the eastern bank, directly in the path of the fire. Others ran to the Ninth Regiment compound. Some feared the fringe of fire they had to cross to reach the safety of the highway rendezvous. Mrs. Wang sent forty trucks to move people from the riverbank, where winds from the west might scorch them to death. Police guided a thousand people to the highway assembly point. She sent thirty trucks to the Ninth Regiment compound to transfer people to the highway crossroads.

There was danger everywhere. Mrs. Wang remembered that forty prisoners had been left in the town jail (among them the miserable Brush Cutter Wang). Mrs. Wang sent a small group to evacuate the prisoners to the highway, where they were guarded by men with rifles. She did not forget the banks — the People's Bank and the Construction Bank. She sent a security detail to truck the money and the bank records to a safe place. After the fire the records helped people whose bankbooks had burned to establish their claims. Those whose money had been tucked in mattresses collected the ashes and unburned bills and turned them in for new bills. Mrs. Wang helped workers in the party-government building bundle up files and got them to safety.

At the post office the clerks refused to leave. They said it was their duty to guard the mail. When the fire crept up the steps they finally agreed to evacuate.

She sent a deputy to try to save the timber storeyard, but the wind beat him there and the yard was afire. He went to the railroad station. That, too, was already burning, the railroad tracks curling and twisting like two fiery sea serpents. The telegraph line had melted. No more link to Tuqing and Amur or anywhere else. No link to the outside world.

At midevening, about 10:00 P.M., the city in darkness, illuminated only by the flames of the burning buildings, the air choked with smoke, Mrs. Wang turned her jeep toward the highway crossroads opposite School Number 1, where she had directed that the people be assembled.

Her jeep slowly picked its way through the debris of the city, scorched by flames from shattered buildings on either side. She found nearly eighteen thousand of the town's twenty-two thousand people gathered on the open ground at the square by the crossroads. They lay on the earth or sat with hands clasped across their knees, quiet, too stunned to move. All about were bundles and precious possessions. Some people rested on blankets. Mothers held their babies to the breast.

The wind was still strong but had lost its initial force. The danger now was that it might shift and whip up the subsiding flames at the edges of this island of safety. Fire still flickered on every side. The people had to be made aware that the danger was not over. Mrs. Wang climbed up on the hood of her jeep and began to shout her warning: "Don't relax! Beware of a shift in the wind!" She knew that many could not hear her words. The wind carried them away. The people were distracted. Some were deaf. She shouted to any party cadres in the crowd to come forward. Three answered her call — one man and two women. She ordered the three to be on the alert. If the wind changed and began to drive flames into the square, they were to try to lead the people to a place of safety. She could not be certain where safety might be found. It depended on the wind. Perhaps they could move farther west into the burned-over hills whence the fire first came. It would be up to them to make a judgment.

As Mrs. Wang was describing the scene at the square, someone in our room made a remark in Chinese. Mrs. Wang laughed. It was the first time since she had begun to talk that her face fleetingly lost its look of total concentration.

Back into the jeep. Back through the city to the eastern edge. Wreckage everywhere, buildings aflame. The streets were clear of people now — all had fled. Back at the Ninth Regiment compound she found Commander Wang Aiwu at the ammunition depot. The fire had passed by the compound, and the situation seemed safe.

Back to town. As she came into the center she went by the guesthouse, the one where we now sat. She saw smoke issuing from a small attached house. She drove to the fire station, but the engine was not there. Her driver had a thought. There was the sewage truck, the one that collected night soil. It was full of sewage and water. He got the truck, drove it to the guesthouse, and pumped the sewage on the flames. It saved the building.

Mrs. Wang looked over the room and said: "Otherwise perhaps you would not be staying in this guesthouse today."

She smiled a tight smile.

On she drove in her jeep. There was still fire everywhere (when it was over, only a handful of buildings was not destroyed). If the people survived, they would need food and clothing. Their homes had burned down. They had lost everything.

"I had to find some food," she said. "I had to find some tents for the people to sleep in."

She went to the fire-control storehouse, a small brick one-story structure near the party and state offices. She had had it checked the day fire broke out at Gulian. She knew there was food and hardtack there. She found the storehouse intact and called over half a dozen fire fighters, who broke down the stout door and the padlocks. Inside were two six-by-twelve-yard tents and a good deal of food — not enough to feed the adults, but, she told herself, at least the children could have something to eat in the morning.

Mrs. Wang swallowed hard and went on with her story.

Now it was after midnight. She had not slept since the day before. (This I learned from someone else.) She made her way across the fire-ravaged western hills to the highway square, where the people had congregated. There she located the police chief and told him that she would hold an emergency meeting of the County Committee at 2:00 A.M. She asked him to try to locate the members.

At the appointed time she and a dozen committee members met with Commander Wang Aiwu at the Ninth Regiment compound. By the still-flickering light of the fires they considered the situation. Mrs. Wang presented her agenda: they must get in food supplies and provide the people with temporary shelter. They must get the burned and injured to hospitals. They must make an accurate account of casualties and check how much housing had been destroyed.

She told her colleagues that the county had lost three forest farms. She did not know how many people had burned to death. She suggested that they take as their slogan "If death comes you must accept it," a sentiment more Confucian than Communist. At 3:00 A.M. she met with about a hundred deputy chiefs and party members. She established a resettlement group, a rescue group, and an investigation group.

It was 4:00 A.M. before her meetings were over. The city was gone. It had been destroyed in the two hours between 7:00 P.M. and 9:00 P.M. Now to care for her people and start the task of restoration. Above all, communications had to be restored.

Exactly when first word of the disaster was transmitted is still not clear. Civilian communications to Tahe from Xilinji failed at 7:10 P.M. on the evening of May 7, when the fire obliterated the telegraph and telephone lines along the railway. Military communications by wireless continued to function. At 9:00 P.M. Commander Wang reported to the governor's office at Harbin that lethal fires were raging at Xilinji and Tuqing. There was a rumor that a telephone line from Hu Wan forest farm somehow remained in operation during the evening of May 7, but no record of any communications via Hu Wan had turned up, and the farm itself was destroyed about that time.

Mrs. Wang sent her first emergency message at 1:10 A.M. on May 8 by the military wireless, to PLA headquarters for the Hinggan district. It simply said that all of Xilinji was "a sea of flames."

At 7:00 A.M. Mrs. Wang made a brief official report. A small wireless transmitter had been located and was set up on the bridge across the river. It was able to transmit a message to the Prefecture Party Committee at Post 18 on the old Manchu Gold Road. The message reported the damage and said preliminary figures showed a casualty toll of two dead and four burned.

Food and tents were urgently needed. The town had no power, no railroad service, no communications. "Immediate help is needed."

I asked her about the casualty figures. Had I heard her correctly — two dead, four burned? She looked down to her lap, and for the first time I thought she was a little flustered. Yes, that was what she reported, that was the total that had been confirmed to that moment. I offered no comment. We both knew that the final figure had been fifty-seven dead and sixty-eight burned.

I still do not know what lay behind the decision to report a figure she had to know was wildly unrealistic. Mrs. Wang made no attempt to explain. It crossed my mind that perhaps other town or county officials had proposed these misleading statistics. Later, when two of Mrs. Wang's colleagues were convicted and sent to prison for their role in handling the catastrophe, my suspicion that others were responsible for these figures was strengthened.

We talked a bit about her background. Her husband, Wang Yongfan, also worked in the forest. He was chief of the county road construction bureau. She had a six-year-old daughter and a mother, fifty-six. Her daughter and mother were at Harbin at the time of the fire.

I was certain that Mrs. Wang must be from the south. She had a small, delicate face, small eyes, artistic hands. She wore standard-issue clothing but conveyed an impression of chic. People of the northern forest region are apt to be big and rugged — the Manchu inheritance. They often have ruddy Mongol cheeks and broad Mongol foreheads, and look like cousins of the

Eskimos or North American Indians, their features seemingly carved by an adze. Mrs. Wang's face was Ming china.

We shook hands. There were tears in my eyes but not, I think, in hers. She knew she had done the right things in May of 1987 and had pride in her understanding of her duty. She had not lost control, not for a moment. It had happened so swiftly. It was over in two hours, the whole city burned down, nothing left but glowing embers and scorched wood, bodies here and there. No one could have predicted the fire. There had not been a moment for a mistake, not an inch of space for misjudgment. Her twenty years in the forest had given her instinctive reactions. They did not fail her. She had done her best for her people, finding tents for the children and guards to watch over the money and the prisoners, all of this as flames one hundred feet high roared down at 40 miles an hour.

Her reward? She was discharged by the provincial government from her office along with a dozen others. It seemed then that there might be more serious charges, but this did not happen. Eventually she was put in charge of county construction, working, it would seem, alongside her husband.

If I had had a medal in my pocket I would have pinned it on her gray jacket. Instead I shook her hand, wished her good fortune, and said good-bye.

I left my room — the one saved from the fire by Mrs. Wang's sewage spraying — and walked out into the beautiful autumn day, air crisp, sky blue, breeze gentle, the kind of day I remember from canoeing in the Arrowhead Forest of Minnesota. Mrs. Wang's words were echoing in my mind as I passed through the streets of Xilinji. The smell of charred wood was hanging in the air, so pervasive I thought I could taste it in the packaged Chinese prune juice I found each day on my breakfast table.

I headed for the hills just south of town, hoping to get a better grasp in my mind of the path of the fire on the night of May 7–8. It was at the foot of these hills that a truck driver had taken the wrong turn, smashed into a tree. Here his daughter was burned to death when she leapt from the wrong side. Here two young relatives, sitting with him in the cab, were badly burned when the gasoline tank exploded. A Xilinji photographer showed me where the girl's body, burned to charcoal, had lain the next morning. He had taken a picture of it and of the body of a party propaganda worker that lay a few yards away.

A footpath led up one hill, narrow as those I had climbed following the trail of Mao Zedong's Red Army on their six-thousand-mile Long March. This was the same kind of "small road," going straight up the hill through the skeleton of the forest, every tree, every bush, every forest plant, every stump black and dead — pines, larch, birch, oak. Toward the top of the hill I angled from the trail, trying to find a better view, trying to find a clearing from which a camera shot could catch the devastation. It was impossible. Desolation was universal. It was like trying to capture an image of the wind. There is no lens wide enough to picture a forest that has just died, black trees extending to the horizon.

Finally I found a place from which I could look down

on Xilinji. I could see clearly the path of the fire's advance over the western hills and across the city, a broad path that left nothing standing except several brick and concrete buildings, burning everything from the railroad in the west to the curve of the river in the east, except — incredibly — a patch of trees still standing near the center of town.

I could find no way of conveying the blackness, the totality, of this world left by the fire, now thinly decorated with wisps of yellow, the ever-resurgent aspens. I wandered in the forest ruin and stumbled on a small clearing where a coffin had been placed, one fire victim brought up the narrow trail and laid to rest in a circle of black trees. You could not see the city here; only black skeletons of trees and the coffin.

A companion exclaimed: "Look at your jacket! It is ruined!" I took it off. The windbreaker bore the imprint of the fire, a feathery design in carbon on my back, the markings of a hundred branches that had touched me as I passed through. Here was the fire imprinted on tan gabardine. I decided to let the markings stay, but by the time I got back to the United States the patterns had rubbed together. Only the faint, persisting scent of forest fire remained to remind me of the death of the trees.

I climbed down the hill and headed for the center of the city and the startling clump of conifers I had seen. It was, I found, a park dedicated to the Hinggan Forest, created when the town was built in 1974. A memorial to the great Green Sea, the square block of untouched trees was not exactly a virgin forest but was filled with miraculous larch and pine, some towering well over a hundred feet, many 150 years old. Here and there, where a tree had been burned in the fire, it had been chopped down and removed. The casualties hardly were to be noticed. Some quirk of wind had preserved this small fragment of the vast forest treasure.

Just beyond the park lay a treeless, bulldozed square, gouged-out raw earth. Here, said the officials of the town, would be erected a children's park with swings, and slides, and merry-go-rounds, and an athletic field. Beside it would be a fire prevention center to educate the public in good forest conduct. In the center they would erect a monument to those who died in the great Black Dragon fire.

VII

Through the Timber Towns: To Ma Lin

AS THE TELEGRAPH lines to the western end of the Black Dragon Forest snapped one by one on the evening of May 7, Commander Ge Xueling at Tahe, on the eastern end, decided he must go west and see for himself what was happening. The loss of communications was more eloquent than oral reports. If fire had destroyed his communications to the west, it must have destroyed a great deal more. Commander Ge was about 150 miles east of what he sensed must be the most critical area, around Xilinji. As chief of forest protection he was, in fact, commander of the battle against the fire.

The commander ordered a helicopter ready at first light, between 4:30 A.M. and 5:00 A.M. on May 8. He slept fitfully, awakening again and again to check the reports. None came in from the west. This was very bad news. The fire must be severe. Equally alarming was the situation in the east, the area within fifty or sixty miles of Tahe. Telephone and telegraph lines still worked, but they brought word that the force of the wind was rising and fires were spreading from the big Pangu forest complex, about forty miles northwest of Tahe.

Tahe, with its population of fifty thousand in town and twenty-five thousand in the surrounding county, was very important to the Black Dragon country. If the Pangu fire kept spreading, it could pose a threat to Tahe. Commander Ge ordered reinforcements to try to make their way westward toward Xilinji and called up more men for Pangu.

By daylight on May 8 Ge could see that he was not going anywhere by helicopter. The smoke was too thick for a helicopter to navigate. The news from the closer fires around Pangu continued to worsen. He decided that it was imperative to assess the situation in Xilinji, and he ordered a fixed-wing plane. But he did not get to Xilinji. Before he could take off the Pangu fire had gone out of control. The government put him in general charge of all the fire fighting. He was given overall command of all the forces, forestry workers, county and provincial resources, and the handful of PLA units already engaged.

"I was responsible for fire precautions," he said, "and fire prevention is my business. I knew that there were going to be big, big problems."

Commander Ge was not the only forest chief trying to get to the west. Three of his colleagues started by train or plane for Xilinji. They ran into obstacle after obstacle. Zhang Ju, a small man with small, hot eyes, got so excited as he told of his efforts he could not sit still; he jumped up, sat down, jumped up again. He had started from Jiagedaqi and managed to get to Tahe, then went west by jeep. The highway was blocked. So he commandeered a locomotive, but the rail line, too, was blocked. He located a jeep on a flatcar, unloaded it, and drove to Amur, a burning timber town of seventeen thousand, seventy-five miles west of Tahe, and then on to Tuqing, forty miles short of Xilinji. Tuqing was, he said, "a sea of fire." He did not make it to Xilinji. At Amur he received a wireless from Commander Ge's headquarters at Tahe telling him to return there. He got back to Tahe at 2:00 A.M. on May 9 to find that town under siege, columns of flame bearing down from the north, the northwest, and the west.

Another forest worker, Zhang Zhuanxiu, couldn't land his helicopter at Tahe, the smoke was so thick and the wind so strong. He managed to get down at Walagan, twenty miles to the west. He saw three red dragons of fire, each twenty miles long or longer, bearing down on Tahe.

The first man from the outside to get to Xilinji was Ma Fu, a veteran forest-resources man. He caught a train at 9:40 P.M., May 7, in Jiagedaqi. It had originated in Qiqihar and was bound for Xilinji. Progress was slow, but somehow the train got through to Amur, a journey of 225 miles to the northwest, by 10:39 A.M. on May 8. Ma Fu had intended to meet local forest officials in Amur, but as the train approached the town he found he was too late. The fire had gotten there first. There wasn't any Amur. The train had to halt well outside the city.

Ma Fu hurried up the tracks and saw that two thirds of the big lumber storage yard near the railroad had burned; the rest was still smoldering. The people he met seemed dazed. Many had fled long since to the riverbank. Some sixty people had burned to death.

Hardly any of the wooden buildings had survived, and fires were still raging. Driven by a 25-mile-an-hour wind, flames neared the oil depot, where a thousand tons of gasoline were stored. Ma Fu joined the local fire fighters and helped them to build a firebreak with a bulldozer. They plowed a circle about thirty feet wide around the depot, creating an island of noncombustible earth across which the flames could not advance.

With a group of officials Ma Fu went on to Tuqing aboard a truck that had been fitted with rail wheels. It made its way along the tracks where the rails had not been twisted into contortions by the flames. They left the tracks and jolted along the roadbed over burning logs and debris. The worst of the fire had passed by, but hot beds of coals were left along the roadbed, their heat reflecting into the truck and causing smoke to curl back from the engine and cab. Half a dozen men were in the body of the truck, lying flat with handkerchiefs to their noses because of the oily smoke. The great danger was that hot embers on the right-of-way might cause the gasoline tank to explode. The driver pushed ahead as fast as he could, but the clutter kept his pace to 8 or 10 miles an hour.

By 4:00 P.M. Ma Fu got to Tuqing. Tuqing no longer existed. It had been burned from end to end, and 103 persons had been killed. Hardly a building still stood. There was no food, no shelter, no drinking water, no communications.

Ma Fu sent a message back down the railroad tracks

to Amur by another forestry official, named Zhang Li. An emergency wireless to the Tahe headquarters was working. Ma Fu reported that Tuqing needed every kind of help urgently. He got back a message to go on to the next and last stop on the railroad — Xilinji, forty miles farther west.

Ma Fu abandoned the truck-on-rails for a jeep and hurried up to Xilinji along the gravel highway. Fires still burned on either side, and the heat was intense. In places the jeep had to leave the road and cut through the burning forest because of fallen logs. Ma Fu arrived in Xilinji about 10:30 P.M., face black with soot, lungs clogged with smoke.

At Xilinji he found the oil depot still surrounded by a briskly burning fire, while exhausted fire fighters kept dousing cotton comforters and water-drenched uniforms, beating the flames with them to keep the fire at a distance.

Ma Fu had gotten instructions by wireless to Amur, forwarded up the line by jeep, to set up an auxiliary fire headquarters at Xilinji. By this time the Black Dragon fire had spread so widely that it was being fought as two fires, the east fire and the west fire, and so the fight would continue for the next thirty days until it was finally extinguished.

I, too, months later, was to make the journey from Tahe to Xilinji and the other timber towns of the Black Dragon country, strung out like beads on an Indian bracelet, north and west of Jiagedaqi — Walagan, Xiu Feng, Pangu, Ma Lin, Amur, Tuqing, Gulian, and Mohe. For the most part these are not Chinese names.

They come from the Er Lunchun, the Mongol tribe that inhabited the area long before the Manchus or Hans or Russians. Most of the timbermen are Han Chinese. There are only remnants of the early Mongols and Manchus.

Anyone who knew northern Wisconsin or northern Minnesota fifty years ago and towns like Hurley, Wisconsin, or Cloquet, Minnesota, would feel at home in the Black Dragon towns. Like their Minnesota cousins they exist for a single purpose, the cutting and processing of conifers. True, the Chinese do not possess the magnificent Norway pines of Minnesota. Most of their cut is Siberian larch, a fine conifer often topping out at a hundred feet, straight as a Greek column, easy to handle, excellent for lumber. But the towns share the rough-cut forest style, the big lumberyards, towering mounds of sawdust, the scent of pitch and resin, men in heavy-belted forest gear, windbreakers, boots, with that slightly rolling gait lumberjacks share with seamen. There are no Last Chance Saloons or cheap dance-halls, no rotgut whiskey, twenty-four-hour poker games, or red-light districts, but there are the timber-laden flatcars; jack pines on the cutover muskeg; gaunt, treeless streets; rumbling trucks; and, in autumn 1987, the clatter of hammers and buzz of construction as rebuilding went forward. At night you wake up to the aching sound of a train whistle fading softly into the distance. It is a rerun of the sights and sounds and smells of my Minnesota boyhood.

The night before we left on our own train journey into the black heart of the dead forest of Hinggan, my three Chinese companions and I were invited — so

urgently we could not refuse — to attend a dance spon-
sored by the party propaganda chief of Tahe and his
wife, an attractive young couple. Ballroom dancing had
been banned by the puritans of the Cultural Revolution
but now was being brought back in the new liberalism
of Deng Xiaoping.

I was reminded of the caves of Yanan, stronghold of
Mao Zedong and his Chinese Red Army in the days of
World War II. There had been Saturday night dances in
a date garden just outside Mao's cave, fox-trots and
even tangos and rumbas danced to records brought in
by American correspondents or, sometimes, music
played by pickup trios of accordionists and Chinese
fiddlers. Chairman Mao, then a skinny, rather awk-
ward figure; Marshal Zhu De, a great bear of a man; the
graceful Zhou Enlai; and other Communist chiefs lum-
bered around the hard clay court in their army boots,
piloted by excited young Chinese women, some of
them Red Army veterans, others recruits just in from
sophisticated Shanghai.

Ours was a young people's dance in this remote region where dancing was still a novelty. It was held in a
dusty assembly hall that doubled as a high-school gym-
nasium. At one end of the hall was a very narrow
platform on which had been placed the biggest tape
player I had ever seen, about the size of a child's coffin.
It blared out Chinese rock and roll and syrupy golden
oldies, adored by contemporary Chinese, young and
old. The tunes sounded almost — but not quite — like
"Old Black Joe" and "Silver Threads Among the
Gold."

Dangling from the ceiling were four crystal chandeliers festooned in ribbons of red and green and gold tinsel left over from celebrations of the past Chinese lunar New Year's. "Happy New Year's Greetings" was spelled out (in Chinese) in cutout kindergarten paper over the platform.

We took seats along the side of the ballroom. Beside us sat eight or ten adults, local party leaders, as I discovered. The men wore dark suits, neat and pressed, one even sporting a white-on-white tie. The ladies wore quite formal dresses, the kind of gowns that might have been seen at afternoon tea dances in Darjeeling in the 1920s. But these were new, not old, gowns, worn very well, white with black or pink touches, decorous but figure-tight, in good taste, with good needlework. The men and women were very attractive in their own style. Beyond the adults sat a dozen young men, of late high-school or early vocational-school age, scrubbed to redness, shaved, hair slicked, each wearing his best (only?) suit, a white shirt and tie, shoes clean and brushed.

Across the room were the girls, clasping and unclasping their hands, in nice dresses, no slacks. The scene was like a teenager's first high-school dance, heavily chaperoned, no one at ease. The party propaganda man and his wife were determined that everyone was going to have a good time, whatever the pain.

The tape recorder boomed a succession of songs. It seemed to require a great deal of attention. Finally the propaganda chief and his wife moved onto the floor, motioning to the other adults to follow. They danced. They danced in the style of Vernon and Irene Castle, high 1920s ballroom dancing, solid fox-trots, Viennese waltzes, polkas, could it be — bunny hugs? wonderful long Valentino glides and the ladies following in romantic swoops. It was a brief turn, then all went back to their seats. The embarrassment of the young people was rising. They squirmed like children at a piano recital.

Stimulated by the urging of the propaganda chief, the party wives, looking as though they were walking on burning coals, approached the silent row where my three companions — Mrs. Wu, Mr. Cui, and Mr. Zhang — and I sat. It was the moment of truth. I admired the courage of these ladies in their finery, walking across the empty floor in spite of their extreme embarrassment and approaching us.

We were in rather heavy forest clothes. The night was frosty. I had on a wool shirt, a wool sweater, and a wool jacket. I wore my heavy country clodhoppers, the ones I wore all through the Black Dragon country, the only shoes I had brought. An extremely proper young woman in rimless glasses, face rigid as a mask, came to me, made a half curtsey, and invited me to dance. I recorded in my notebook: "A very prim lady of 36 or 40, bandbox dress, nice shoes, her heart in her mouth, came forward and invited me to dance."

I am a nondancer, but I could not let this courageous young lady down. We took the floor, stiffly extending our arms, and, with a foot of air between us, sedately progressed across the floor. She said not one word, nor did I. I guessed that she might be a schoolteacher. My companions succumbed to similar invitations. Mrs. Wu protested valiantly but finally did a quick turn, then returned to her chair.

All through the dance I felt the eyes of the boys and girls on us in agony. Our performance had been preceded by an introduction in which the propaganda chief told them how important we were, how I had come to Tahe all the way from America, and the others from Beijing. If there had been a hole they would have crawled into it.

Finally, several couples of what I took to be young marrieds came onto the floor. They were good dancers, not as good as the chief, but their style approached that of the 1960s. Very shyly, two pair of girls in their late teens began to dance, and a solemn, self-conscious pair of boys. None held a candle to an elderly couple who I imagined to be old cadres sent to the Black Dragon Forest to rusticate during the Cultural Revolution and who had not bothered to return to Shanghai. She was dressed in a well-cut gray tailored suit of the style worn by important elderly cadres, the widow of Zhou Enlai or Zhu De, for example. He wore a slightly old-fashioned dark business suit. There was an air of musty elegance about this pair, and they danced a good foxtrot, their rhythm good, their timing good, their pleasure in their skill charmingly evident. This was, I thought, like a YMCA mixer, a reminder of my college days.

Somehow I related the dance to the fire, an evidence of the spirit of this distant forestland. It was a land of youth, young towns, young people, a young frontier, and these were people of China's surging young generation, their enthusiasm not singed by the terror of the fire. They were like the aspens. The conifers might die, but they would survive. No backward look.

Yet, in one manner, they differed from all the other surging millions of young China. That autumn every youngster, so it seemed, from Chengdu and Guangdong to the dusty reaches of Shaanxi, was singing Shanghai's newest hit. It was called "Fire in Winter," and it was at the top of every hit parade:

You are like a fire in winter,
Raising flames that warm my heart.
Whenever you pass by your flame lights me up.
Your big eyes are bright and sparkling,
Like the brightest star in the sky,
I haven't told this yet to you,
But I know you like me with all your heart.

No one among the hot-blooded youngsters of the Black Dragon land wanted to compare their love to fire. It was like mentioning rope in the house of a man who had been hanged. I traveled the Black Dragon from one end to the other. I never heard a strain of "Fire in Winter."

We left the dance early. At 4:00 A.M. we would take the train from Tahe and move arrow-straight through the heart of the fire zone to Xilinji, where it had all started. Or had it? More and more I was becoming aware that this was not a single fire. It was not just the miserable Brush Cutter Wang who had started it. It had many origins, and the greatest single factor had been the wind.

We drove in darkness through the Tahe streets, seeing few lights, no cars, but as we neared the railroad station we sensed a shuffling in the blackness that grew louder until we reached the station. We found it jammed inside, while another hundred people outside waited for the 4:00 A.M. train to Xilinji. Stars powdered the broad sky. There was a waning moon. Frost numbed our hands and froze our spines. These were workers of the forest going west on their assignments: men and women; young men and women; some PLA men; some construction workers; a young man with a guitar slung over his arm like a Red Army man's Mauser during the Long March, a tape player as big as a 1930s wireless transmitter hunched over his shoulders; pretty eighteen-year-old women in long sheepskin coats, skin outside, wool inside, red shoes with high heels; girls in red windbreakers, red jackets, red coats, red, red, red, the color of the season. And, of course, peasant women with teakettles and bundles, baskets and babies. The station was a clutter of sleeping bodies. They had been waiting a long time, slumped on wooden benches, crumpled on the cement floor, workers in padded jackets, peasants with white cotton bags.

I could see already the first faint veins of red in the eastern sky. I thought how the glow of fire four or five months earlier had encarmined the heavens. We took our places in a hard car, a very hard car, three abreast, facing three abreast on the seat opposite, bundling heavy horse blankets across our laps, every space in the car filled with the sleeping and the half-asleep, across from me a peasant woman who had survived the fire at Xilinji, going home, sick-stomach, perhaps pregnant, fearful that she would vomit. A foot away, I worried, too.

The rose faded in the sky, and clear light opened my eyes to the landscape, at first not burned over, at least not burned over recently, a mixed forest, green and red and yellow, patches of charcoal burn here and there, a succession of small forest settlements, then fewer and fewer intervals between the patches until there were no longer patches — just endless burn, black, black, black, endless black, black hills to the west and south, black settlement after settlement, town after town, burned.

The ride from Tahe to Xilinji takes seven hours, seven hours of black. I got tired of looking. It was all the same. All burn. I had heard so much about the forest, had heard so many talk of what had happened. Now I could begin to put what I had heard against the background of the endless distances where once nothing could be seen but the sea of green.

With daylight and our first brief station halt I saw something I had never before seen in China, land of fresh green-painted railroad cars and fine old black-painted locomotives with red-painted wheels: the paint on the hard-seat coach in which we were traveling was blistered and peeling. At first I did not make the connection. Then I realized what it meant. This was a car that had gone through the fire. It had been saved, but there had not been time yet to paint over the scars.

"Yes," said Zhang Yuanxiu, who fought the fire at Walagan, "it was hot all right. Our hard hats melted. We poured water on them to keep them from catching afire."

We moved along the Greater Hinggan Range, forest town after forest town, the scenes of the tragedies with which I had been living for days. This was where it happened.

Walagan, Ma Lin, Amur, Tuqing. Some I had seen already but not in sequence, not as links in the fiery chain.

Ma Lin . . . its ruins a black scorch, workmen putting up long rows of one-story brick housing, divided like sausage links into two- or three-room houses. On a hill the big-dish TV receiver newly in place, trucks crawling through the cluttered streets. Ma Lin . . . This was the town where Zhang Zhangxi of the Walagan Forest Company almost lost his life. A third of his company of ninety-one fire fighters was burned, seven of them, including himself, very seriously. One fire fighter died of his burns. He had worn a shirt made of synthetic fiber. Sparks hit the shirt, and it went in one big puff, burning the man terribly. The other fire fighters wore forestry-issue cotton shirts. No problem. Synthetics burn much faster, so Zhang said.

Zhang was thirty-two years old and a twelve-year veteran of the Forest Service. He had brought his ninety-one men up to Ma Lin in three trucks, the wind blowing at 30 feet a second, he estimated. He spotted a woman and three men surrounded by fire and tried to break through the circle. The fire was moving so swiftly they had only two minutes for the rescue. Two men were saved, one man and the woman lost. Zhang was badly burned. The worst time had been trying to get from Ma Lin to Tahe in a truck with other injured. It moved very, very slowly. The smoke was thick, the road covered with burning litter, flames leaping from both sides of the road. The fire exhausted the oxygen in the air, and breathing became hard. When the truck engine stopped it could hardly be restarted. The flames curled over the road like "the breaking surf of the sea."

Zhang Zhangxi was not optimistic about the regeneration of the forest. "It will take a hundred and eighty years to bring back the big trees," he said.

Three buildings still stood at Ma Lin, a school, an office, and a garage. The rest was gone. Officials said only ten people had died and thirty burned, but I took this to be an underestimate. I could count almost that number of casualties in the handful of people with whom I talked.

Ma Lin . . . That was where a housewife named Bai Yuan spent the evening of May 7 alone with her two children, a boy of eleven and a girl of eight. Her husband and most of the men in town had gone to Tuqing. That's where the men of Ma Lin, of Amur, had gone to battle the flames.

Ma Lin was perhaps forty miles from Tuqing, far away from the fire danger. Usually Bai Yuan stayed up watching her favorite Chinese soap opera on TV. But the program wasn't on that Thursday evening, so she had gone to bed. Nothing to worry about. Tuqing was far away, and a nearer fire at Pangu, she had heard, had been brought under control.

At about 11:00 P.M. a loud noise awakened her. It was the wind ripping the corrugated iron roof off her house. The sky was red with the approaching flames. She threw on her clothes and ran out, a child holding each hand. As she ran for the highway her boy, Yang Yuming, slipped from her grasp. The fire passed over like a wild barrage. Two hours later she found her son, his face burned, but not badly, crouched beside the road. He had run away in fright.

I talked to Yuming outside a new house that had been built for the family in Ma Lin. It was a bright autumn day, and he was playing with his friends, a slingshot made of twisted wire in his hands. His faded sweatshirt bore in English the legend "LET'S PLAY SOC- CER BALL." I asked him what had happened the night of the fire. "I forgot," he replied. I persisted. All he would say was "I'm not afraid of fire." The memory of the night when he had run away into the darkness had vanished, but perhaps not entirely. I asked how he was doing in school. He would not answer. One of his friends volunteered: "Not so well." A fat lady who lived next door listened impassively as we talked. Someone said she had lost 6,000 yuan, burned in the fire. But the government replaced it. "We have a lot of ten-thousand-yuan families around here," an official said. "A 10,000-yuan family" is a euphemism for a rich family at the village level.

Another Ma Lin fire fighter sent from Walagan was Chen Shouwen, of Company Number 4. A droopy mustache, a cap, and a neat jacket gave him a resem- blance, I thought, to a professor of English. He had set off for Ma Lin about 10:00 P.M. on May 7. He'd seen no signs of anything wrong. There had been a little smoke about 5:00 P.M., but nothing worth notice. When he approached Ma Lin he saw a vast fire bearing down on his truck and realized that Ma Lin had already burned. As he leapt to the ground he guessed that the flames towered two hundred feet above him.

"I thought I might be dead," he said. "The fire was all around me. I fell down and the fire swept by. Then I knew I would survive. My face and hands were burned. My clothes were on fire. I threw off my jacket and my cotton work clothing. I was left with a sweater and a shirt. My trousers were scorched."

All around on the highway lay the burned and dead. No communications. People were running for their lives. But Chen saw no one come out of the village of Ma Lin. He lay still until the morning. He found it hard to breathe, and he had almost been blinded. His eyes were singed.

When I talked with him about coming up to Ma Lin and seeing the towers of fire, the sound of the wind still reverberated in his ears, he said. The sound was loud and strong; it was the sound of fire, the sound of fire, shouting.

VIII

Black Beard

WHEN I TOLD PEOPLE in China that I had been up to the Black Dragon country, the question was always: "Did you meet Black Beard?" He was the hero of the Hinggan Forest fire.

Black Beard is Wu Changfu, forty-six years old, a deputy division commander of the PLA. By the time I met him, in late September 1987, he was smooth-shaven as a choirboy; the stubby black beard grown during twenty-five days of fighting the great fire, in violation of PLA regulations requiring soldiers to shave each day, was gone. Having seen his bearded portrait in the Revolutionary Military Museum, I did not recognize this small, boyish man with his tight grin as China's hero of the year.

Commander Wu Changfu was not the first army commander to get to the fire, but he was the one the public remembered from appearances on TV, interviews, and photographs in the press.

The Black Dragon country is at all times as stuffed

with soldiers as a raisin cake with raisins. Since Sino-Soviet relations became hostile in the late 1960s there have been many troops tucked away in the deep woods. In addition to garrison troops (like Commander Wang Aiwu's Ninth Regiment at Xilinji) there were road and construction outfits like the Second Battalion. Some two thousand PLA men in thirty-two companies were working in the forest when the fire broke out. They were the first to get into action.

The decision to bring in a mass of PLA regulars was made by the State Council in Beijing very quickly, when the reports on May 8 disclosed the scope of the disaster and the danger of a holocaust.

Commander Ge Xueling, as temporary commander at Tahe, was in the thick of the fire fighting. I asked him when he first saw a possibility of bringing the fire under control. It came, he said, with the decision to bring in the PLA and hundreds of expert Forest Service fighters from Inner Mongolia and other areas.

"For the first time," he said, "I began to see the possibility that we could bring it under control. Before the PLA came in the fire continued to spread, only more slowly. But it was still burning with great intensity."

Black Beard spoke to me not in the Black Dragon country nor at his old command post at Harbin. We talked in an airy room of the College of Military Science, to which he was assigned after the fire. It is located in the western hills of Beijing, where many PLA institutions are to be found, in a spacious, tight-security region of gray brick buildings, peaceful streets, little traffic, pine-lined roadways, and flowering shrubs, a California atmosphere that reminded me a bit of Santa

Barbara, the gentle slopes of the western hills in the background.

Commander Wu greeted me with a perfunctory grin and a glance at the TV cameras that had become so much a part of his recent life. He smiled another tight grin when I admitted I had not recognized him without his black stubble.

What, he asked, could he do for me?

"Tell me all about the great fire and your experience," I said. He demurred lightly. He had told the story so often there was nothing more to tell, he said; then he plunged into it. As I scribbled my notes I looked him over carefully. He was small and compact but, I thought, very tough, a bundle of nerves and muscle, hair cropped but head not shaven (as PLA officers' often are), fit and alert. He pulled out a pack of cigarettes and lighted one as he started to talk. It was the first of three he smoked in a two-hour conversation. His lips formed a thin line when he pressed them together during the pauses that punctuated his story. He spoke in a loud, pejorative voice, as though addressing recruits on a parade ground, sometimes barking out words one by one as if spitting bullets. I didn't think he possessed an ounce of grace. All business. He was on the way up, and that was all that counted.

As so often in Chinese interviews we sat in big armchairs, side by side, with a little table for tea and ashtrays between us. The commander addressed his words to the TV cameras and the handful of people sitting in front of him, glancing over to me when he stopped talking to let the translator interpret his machine-gun bursts.

Black Beard went a bit beyond normal expectations in lavishing praise on the party, the government, and the State Defense Committee for aid and support of his efforts. Only when I asked some specific questions did he mention the name of any military individual other than his subordinates.

Black Beard and his division had been at Harbin before the fire broke out. At 6:40 P.M. on May 8 he got orders to move north. By 9:00 P.M. on May 8, Black Beard said, his men (the First Battalion of the division) were packed and ready to move, but it was another two hours before rail transport could be assembled. It is a bit over five hundred miles from Harbin to Tahe, and Black Beard had time to think about his assignment. His men had been loaded so fast most of them hadn't brought any clothes or equipment, not even money. They had rations for three days. Everything, Black Beard said, was supposed to be supplied in the fire zone. At station stops white-aproned girls were selling Popsicles, but the men didn't have a feng in their pockets. An old peasant woman was selling eggs for thirty-five feng. "I'd like to give them to you," she told the men, "but I had to buy them myself."

Black Beard was lavish in his praise for the support his men got from local citizens. They had started without fire-fighting equipment, without shovels, picks, or axes. All of this was provided, he said, by the provincial and regional governments.

Black Beard's instructions were clear. He was to defend Tahe and Xiu Feng, just to the northwest, from the fire. He must keep it from crossing the east-west railroad line, Tahe to Mohe, and the Huma River, and he

must prevent it from moving into the virgin forest reserves to the south.

As Black Beard told his story the TV crews switched
their lights on to record segments, particularly those
passages in which he praised the party and government. The lights clicked on and off like part of a pinball
game.

Black Beard admitted that he and his men had little
or no experience in fighting forest fires. As a youngster
he once acted as a guide to some PLA men fighting a
fire, and he had been deputy commander of a company
once assigned to a mountain fire. Not much, he conceded, but he was given everything he needed to fight
the fire, and he proved to be a quick learner. You could
not go into battle without guns and ammunition, he
said, and you could not fight a fire without food, water,
and equipment.

At Tahe the local officials put him in charge of PLA
units. He had his own battalion, and although he did
not point it out to me, there was already in place one of
the finest regiments in the PLA, led by Political Com-
missar Gao Sizhong. These seven hundred men had
been rushed from the Huzhong forest farm, southwest
of Tahe, in open cattle cars in a snowstorm. They had
left so fast they had neither overcoats nor equipment.
Part of an outstanding PLA division founded during the
war against the Japanese, they had been led then by the
famous marshal Chen Yi in the Meng-Liang-Gu cam-
paign. The regiment had been first across the Yangtse
River to occupy Nanjing and was renowned for its ability to endure hardship, for marching long distances, if
necessary, on empty stomachs. These men were a

priceless asset in the fire battle. Their unit had been stationed in the forest zone and was one of the first to join the fire fighting.

Black Beard and his men got to Tahe at 4:46 P.M. on May 9. He left a deputy to off-load his troops and hurried to local headquarters. The day was dark, and he thought it looked like rain. He did not realize the sun had been darkened by the smoke. The fire was now about twenty miles to the northwest. The wind was force 5, about 20 miles an hour, and blowing from northwest to southeast, enveloping the city in thickening smoke. The fire front was halfway between Xiu Feng and Walagan. All able-bodied men in town were fighting it. Old women and children had been left behind. If the fire got loose, few would escape.

After telling his deputy to bring the troops to Xiu Feng as fast as he could, Black Beard got into a jeep and headed for the fire. He was armed with a good local map. There were, he discovered, four fires, big ones — four fire dragons. One was three miles long and throwing flames and fiery debris three hundred feet into the air, headed straight for Xiu Feng. The Xiu Feng forest men and local officials, according to Black Beard, couldn't decide what to do. Some wanted to send his men into a frontal assault. Others wanted to slip a detachment behind the fire and attack from the rear. Others favored an attack from the sides. Some favored a backfire. The fire was only five miles from Xiu Feng, and it was a hard call for the inexperienced Black Beard. The great fear was that if the fire swept across Xiu Feng Forest, it would roar down on Tahe.

Xiu Feng was the only barrier north of the city, and

the specific line Black Beard had to hold was Forest Road Number 2, a logging access road. If the fire leapt over that road, the way to Tahe, ten miles to the southeast, was clear. There was no other road, highway, or river line on which a stand could be made. Losing Tahe, with its large population and concentration of state offices and facilities, would be a terrible blow. The loss of Forest Road Number 2 would almost certainly lead to the destruction of the Xinlin Forest Bureau just to the south and of the priceless Huzhong national forest reserve, slightly southwest of Tahe. If the fire spread to the east, it would devour the Han Jia Yuan forest farm.

"This was the heart of the Hinggan Forest," Black Beard said. He grew excited as he talked, moving his hands like an actor. "If the human heart is lost the human being cannot survive. If a forest loses its heart it cannot survive. It would affect the whole ecological balance of the Black Dragon region." Thus, he said, it was clear to him that his first task was to defend the Number 2 road. He said that by the time his men took their position on the road, residents were fleeing Tahe like rats leaving a sinking ship. They were trying to get away by any means, certain that Tahe would be destroyed.

Black Beard said he had found himself in a dangerous dilemma. He had had no experience with a big fire. He could see no way of protecting the Number 2 road except by a backfire. A backfire is a fundamental weapon employed in fighting forest fires. In simplest form it is a fire that is deliberately set in the path of an advancing forest fire. It is a controlled blaze over a tract of land lying ahead of the fire. A line of men with blowers and beaters keeps it from spreading out of control. When the forest fire hits the freshly burned-over spot it is halted. It has no fuel to keep going. There is, of course, danger that a backfire may get out of control and simply add to the ferocity of the original wildfire. But experienced foresters use it as one of their basic control methods.

Black Beard realized that any wind shift could turn the fire onto his own men, engulfing them before sweeping down on Xiu Feng and Tahe.

"Then I might be labeled a saboteur," he said, "and the casualties would be heavy." Nonetheless, he decided on the gamble and ordered his men to start work on a backfire. At 11:27 A.M., May 10, he got an urgent summons to report to Tahe. The wind, he said, was at force 5 (about 20 miles an hour) and irregular, dropping to force 3 and shifting direction.

Before he left for Tahe an officer advised him that another, smaller fire had been put out. Not all of Black Beard's men were happy to see him go. If something happened while he was in Tahe, who would take responsibility? He assured them he would take the blame and would get back as fast as he could.

At Tahe he reported his decision to try a backfire. Some opposition developed, but he got the support of the vice governor and the deputy forestry minister and rushed back, arriving at 4:00 A.M. on May 11. Black Beard insisted that his men still needed three more agonizing hours before they could touch off the backfire at 7:00 A.M. He massed his men to guard against mishaps, and the fire was a success.

Later that day or the next a gust of wind set the fire

going again. It took three more days before Black Beard got it back under control. Only then could he report that Forest Road Number 2 was safe and secure.

At one point (Black Beard did not mention this) two of his regiments were surrounded by fire. Professional foresters rescued them.

Black Beard's version did not match the way other fire fighters explained what had happened on Forest Road Number 2. In fact, their account was at total variance with Black Beard's — and much less dramatic.

According to this version, a skilled group of forest men had made a stand on Forest Road Number 3, a few miles farther away from Xiu Feng and Tahe. With four hundred men from Pangu and a thousand from Xiu Feng, they believed they could hold the line here. This was before Black Beard had arrived on the scene. They built a firebreak with the aid of some professional fire fighters. It was half a mile long and thirty feet wide, and they thought it should protect the Number 3 road. But the wind suddenly rose, and the fire rushed forward in twenty-five-foot leaps. Some two hundred of the fire crew were surrounded within an enclave a mile long and half a mile wide.

Zhang Zhangjai is a big, slow-moving forest machine-shop boss with a great brush of black hair that sags over his forehead. He pushed it back with a lazy gesture as he told me of his part in this crisis. Zhang and another forestry section chief, named Du Jinxiang, happened to be outside the encirclement where the fire fighters were trapped. They found two trucks. They had great difficulty starting the motors because the fire had so reduced the oxygen content of the air. Finally they got the vehicles going and drove straight through the circle of fire. Flames reached out from both sides, but they got through. Zhang and Du piled as many of the trapped workers onto the trucks as could be crammed in. They got a hundred men on the two vehicles, leaving a hundred behind. They found a place where the fire seemed a bit thinner and roared through, almost blinded by the smoke. On the highway they were still not safe. Fire followed them on both sides.

"Some people probably were burned when we went through the circle of fire," Zhang admitted. "But there was nothing else we could do." They made a second crash entry to the enclave, loaded up the rest of the fire fighters, and got them out.

Then they brought the workers down to the Number 2 road, where thirteen professional fire fighters assisted in setting the backfire. They had burned a two-mile barrier in front of the advancing flames by 9:00 P.M. on May 10 — a full ten hours before Black Beard's men, as he claimed, had set off the backfire that turned the tide. Tahe, the professionals said, was now "at least 80 percent safe."

Discrepancies in accounts of such complex crises are inevitable. But the contradictions between Black Beard's account and that of the professionals were not likely to be resolved. Black Beard took full credit for saving Tahe. The professionals suggested that the city had been saved before Black Beard got his men deployed. Black Beard's propensity for brash talk apparently was well known. He told me his superior officer had warned him to mind his tongue or he would be in "deep trouble."

What really counted — however it was achieved — was that the stand at Road Number 2 was a genuine victory. No soldier died in the battle, although a cook lost his life. Exhausted by ten days of continuous duty, he fell asleep in a parked truck. The driver started the engine. A broken exhaust pipe leaked carbon monoxide through the floor. Six other men were overcome but revived.

It was during these first hectic days that Black Beard stopped shaving. His beard grew more and more black. Sometimes he went two days without eating. Once the fire singed his beard and hair. He got no sleep. Thirty-two of his commanders and soldiers were commended for their battle to save Road Number 2.

By this time Black Beard had fourteen hundred troops at Xiu Feng, eight hundred local fire fighters, forty blowers with skilled operators, and forty trucks to shift the men from front to front.

On May 13 Li Peng, the vice premier charged with ultimate responsibility for combating the fire, arrived at Tahe. The situation was still far from clear. Black Beard's tactics had worked, but only temporarily, and a big new fire was occupying all his men and all his energy.

Li Peng was aware that the fire might yet break through the Xiu Feng area and burn down Tahe. He knew that the fire in the western sector was still in precarious balance. He called the cadres and PLA chiefs, including Black Beard, to the Tahe headquarters to examine the situation. The fire was spreading, if more slowly, both east and west. Li Peng ordered the lines held. The fire was not to cross Road Number 2 or invade Xiu Feng or Tahe. It was not to cross the Huma River or reach the banks of the Black Dragon. It must be stopped. He formally ordered the fire front divided. Black Beard was given command of the east sector, and (I had to pry this information out of the beard) army general Ma Fengtong was named commander of the west sector. Ma was a full general, Black Beard a division commander. This was Black Beard's only reference to the man with whom he shared command of the Black Dragon battle, a man his senior if not his superior. Black Beard was very much a young man on the make.

General Ma Fengtong did not possess Black Beard's flair. He was a man in his late fifties. He shaved every day. He went about his task of putting out the fires in the western zone in a routine if not bureaucratic way. People in the western zone hardly saw him and later complained that he spent his time in his headquarters at Xilinji, not out on the scene of the battle.

Li Peng was not satisfied merely to receive the commanders' reports. He had to visit the front line and see for himself. He flew by helicopter to Xilinji. Visibility was poor, but he saw the destruction in Amur, Tuqing, and Xilinji and even went up to Mohe, in spite of protests by officials who thought he should not go so close to the Soviet border. "I must see the whole area," said Li Peng. That was that.

With his designation as east front commander, Black Beard received more authority, more troops, and four helicopters. He had been, he said, traveling three hundred to four hundred miles a day in his jeep. Now he converted a copter to his personal use, installing a two-way command wireless. He practically lived in the helicopter.

There was plenty to occupy him. When Black Beard got his command there were, he estimated, seventeen major fires raging and 231 serious fire sites. He was constantly on the move, trying to carry out his orders: prevent the fire from breaking through to the Black Dragon River or across the Tahe-Nenjiang north-south highway. More than 25,000 PLA men had been brought into the fire area; apparently a bit more than half were under Black Beard's command. By the time the fire was quenched, in early June, there were 36,000 to 40,000 troops, two armies, and many special units engaged in fire operations. Exactly how the forces were split was not clear from Black Beard's account. Nor did he describe how he coordinated his work with that of the western front commander. Troops were, however, constantly moved from one danger spot to another.

Wang Heping took part in the battle under Black Beard's command. He was a political officer in an outfit designated 81412. On the afternoon of May 12 he was playing basketball in Harbin with some medical personnel. His team had just lost the ball and was trying to get it back when an orderly came with word that they were to leave immediately for the north. They departed from Harbin at 2:00 A.M., reached Pangu at 1:00 A.M. on May 14, and from there, on orders of Black Beard, moved north to Ershierzhan, Post 22 on the Gold Road, east of the Pangu River.

It was a sunny day, but the sunshine was gray with

Wang Zhaowin, the heroic thirty-six-year-old mayor of Xilinji, led a valiant fight to save her town but lost her job after the fire in a political housecleaning.

Yang Yuming, eleven years old, with his slingshot outside his new house in Ma Lin. He ran away from his mother in fright the night the fire struck, and the trauma has wiped details of the experience from his mind.

Zhou Jinbao, fourteen, was a hero of the fire at Ma Lin. He failed in an effort to save his mother from the flames but led several neighbors to safety, suffering terrible burns and almost losing his life.

Commander Ge Xueling, born in the northern forests, top professional in China's fight against the Black Dragon fire. His
name, in Chinese, translates as "study the forest." He has
devoted his life to fulfilling the meaning of his name.

Soldiers beat at the fire with branches torn from nearby trees.

Wang Yufeng, the eighteen-year-old worker whose carelessness started the first blaze at the Gulian forest farm, which touched off the Black Dragon conflagration. Shown here in the courtroom, he received a sentence of six years and six months in prison for negligence.

This mechanical brush cutter is similar to the one Wang handled so sloppily on May 6, 1987. The cutter pictured here is being operated by a worker at the Gulian forest farm, where Wang was a temporary employee.

Bao Guorong, a senior official in the Amur forest complex, was charged with fleeing by car with his wife, leaving a thousand people in peril. He was sentenced to three years in prison.

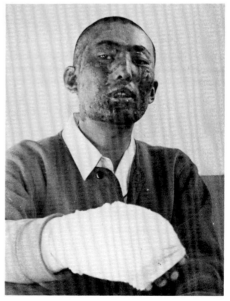

Han Gaolin, army soldier, was badly burned fighting the fire.

The ruins of Xilinji, in Mohe County, a town of twenty-two thousand
at the western end of the fire area.

smoke. By May 15 Wang's unit was ten miles from the Black Dragon River and the Soviet frontier. Here they fought a fire, swatting it with branches. Branches were the chief weapon of the ordinary fire fighter, branches or heavy swatters made of twigs. The fire was still burning on the morning of the sixteenth. The wind rose and the fire started to move. They chased it more than twenty miles, throwing away all their equipment as they ran — clothes, food, everything. At nightfall the temperature dropped to 25 degrees Fahrenheit. They had neither coats nor blankets nor food for twenty-four hours. Cold, hunger, and exhaustion — that was what they remembered about the fire. They got to the banks of the Black Dragon. No Russians were in sight. The Soviet gunboats had abandoned their patrol, fearful of being set on fire. "One curious thing," Wang said. "As the soldiers fought they shouted a lot. They shouted at the fire."

Everywhere Wang looked there were burned houses, only their chimneys standing, and piles of ashes where there had been cottages or shops. In one ruin he saw an iron safe. He poked at it and the door fell off. Inside there was a plate of melted coins. Everyone had fled the village. He couldn't remember its name, but judging from the map, it was probably Kai Ku Kong, east of the junction of the Pangu and Black Dragon rivers. He and his men opened the door of an earthen cellar. They were almost paralyzed by the fetid smell of rot. Nearby Wang saw the charred railings of a pigsty. No pigs remained, but three sets of pigs' teeth gleamed like ivory in charcoal jaws.

IX

"Mom Didn't Make It"

THE STRUGGLE to save the Black Dragon Forest was far from over. Black Beard was becoming an expert on fire-fighting technology. He had never seen a power blower before the fire; now he worked with blowers every day. Without an expert operator, he said, you could not use them effectively. The blower he and his men used ran on a one-cylinder, single-cycle gasoline engine with a magnetic generator, which started easily. The model made in Sian weighed sixty pounds, including a full tank of gasoline. It could be used directly as a blower or connected to a chemical fire extinguisher and at six feet, face-to-face with a fire, could hardly be beat for turning the flames back with a powerful blast of air. He had not, he said, been able to use blowers well in his first big encounter at Xiu Feng. I should have asked him more about that. The professionals who said they were fighting the Xiu Feng blaze before Black Beard got there told me they found blowers a great help.

"It is a dangerous job," Black Beard said. "All the

men using the blowers suffered burned hands, but they didn't complain and went on fighting the fire."

I asked him to explain how he had been able, as he asserted, to keep the fire from reaching the Black Dragon River; I had heard from others that the fire did indeed reach the river. He said that would be a very long talk; even an hour would not be long enough. But he managed to finish his story in half an hour. I thought he might be worrying about being late for lunch. As it turned out, he never did make clear exactly how the fire allegedly was kept from the river, but he did reveal that after he had thought the fires virtually extinguished they suddenly sprung up again in very dangerous shape.

Apparently it was in this last period that the threat to the river line arose close to the border between the east and west zones, that is, along the Tahe-Mohe county line. The main threat, Black Beard insisted, was on the west side of the line, not in his district. He was very sure about that.

Since a number of the points he mentioned can be located only on fine-detail maps, to which I didn't have access, it was not possible to confirm his version. But there was little doubt that this last phase was one of the most dangerous episodes of the entire fire. Jack Minor, the Canadian fire fighter based in Jiagedaqi, was certain the Chinese were very worried that the Russian fire would leap across the river at this time.

Black Beard had told me that the fire in the east zone had been put out by noon of May 23: "All the visible fires were out."

But nature had a trick in store. On May 22 a fire

north of the east-west highway from Tahe to Mohe broke across the road at Wahuang. This fire threatened one of the most important nature reserves in the Black Dragon region, the Huzhong reserve, near the forest farm from which the crack battalion of Chen Yi's old division had been brought in even before Black Beard's arrival.

Fire fighters started an emergency firebreak. They did everything they could think of to keep the fire from boiling across the railroad and into the virgin timber.

Chinese forest specialists had been experimenting for some time with exotic means of extinguishing fires. The time had come to pull out all the stops. A special gun had been devised to fire oxygen-devouring chemicals into the fire. If oxygen could be removed from the environment, the fire could be snuffed out. These experiments failed to stop the fire.

As Black Beard observed, the most effective element in depriving a fire of oxygen is rain, but not a light drizzle. A fire will simply extract oxygen from the light mixture and burn even harder. What was needed was a heavy rain. The Chinese knew of the many futile efforts made in Canada and the United States at cloud seeding. Rain in nature occurs when the moisture of clouds is condensed into water, which then falls to the ground in drops. Cloud seeding employs chemical agents to produce condensation. Dry ice or such chemicals as silver iodide are sprayed into clouds in the hope that they will cause temperature changes, which produce condensation. Usually the chemicals are sprinkled from airplanes flying through clouds. The technique is used only as a last resort since scientists are not yet convinced it really works.

In the crisis at the end of May, when huge new fires arose in almost inaccessible areas, the Chinese turned to cloud seeding. On May 25–26 some four thousand shells of dry ice were fired into the clouds by PLA artillery. Planes from the base at Qiqihar overflew the area, sprinkling dry ice and silver iodide. The experiment, Black Beard asserted, was successful. A moderate rain fell. Whether it would have fallen anyway none could say. What was important was that the fire died out.

The Chinese did not employ the water-dumping technique, a favorite tactic of American and Canadian fire fighters. They did not possess the modified tanker planes, water-carrying helicopters, or scooper planes developed by the Canadians.

Hardly had the Huzhong fire been stifled than another peril arose on May 25 — a huge fire, possibly started by lightning, broke out in the Xiao Bai Dala Mountains, in a virgin forest with no access roads and no routes for planes or helicopters bringing in forest crews. When discovered, it had already burned more than six thousand acres. There was, Black Beard said, no way to get at it. This tract of land was at the boundary line of Tahe and Mohe counties about twelve miles north of the railroad, not far from the Black Dragon River and the twenty-sixth post on the Gold Road. Again the cannon and the planes were deployed. This time a heavy rain fell for two days and one night, extinguishing the fire. Again, no one could be certain that the magic bullets had brought the moisture. This chemical attack was carried out on June 1, Deputy Forestry Minister Xu Youfang reported. In view of the long controversy in the west over seeding techniques, I asked if he planned to make a report to some scientific forestry journal. He hadn't thought of that, he said, but it sounded like a good idea.*

These outbreaks presented the last critical threats. I was convinced that the Chinese believed their chemical warfare had produced results. The fire was declared officially ended June 2, the day after the second chemical assault and two weeks after Black Beard had first thought the fire was out.

From Black Beard's account I could not determine whether he considered the last outbreaks part of his fire-fighting responsibility or whether, as his language indicated, he put responsibility for them on the west sector. But it was, after all, one fire and one country.

Not all the forest men in the Black Dragon country echoed the cheers that rang out for Black Beard's exploits. There were those who said he was too quick to employ backfires, that too much of the forest reserve had been burned in his efforts to control the terrible blazes. But this was not an opinion shared by the government, the PLA, or the general public. To them the words Black Dragon would instantly evoke the name Black Beard, hero of the holocaust.

I had been told in the forest country that some remarkable films had been taken by a crew of the August First studio, the PLA film company, which happened to be

---

*As of January 1, 1989, no such report had been published.

in Xilinji when the fire broke out. The crew, I was told, had gone to Hinggan to make a picture called *Ba Nu Tuo Tiang*, about eight heroic Chinese maiden guerrillas who drowned themselves in Mudan (Poppy) Lake, having fired their last bullets at the Japanese. Like many stories of the Black Dragon fire, the happy coincidence of this crew's location was part true, part not. The crew had indeed gone to the forest to film at Mudan Lake, but the site is far to the east of the fire zone. What actually happened was that the PLA rushed its best documentary crew to the Hinggan.

It was this crew, headed by Yang Gangyan, the PLA's top documentary newsman, that filmed the fire. They got to the scene just after Black Beard. They flew in a plane carrying wind blowers and shot everything from Tahe to Xilinji — everywhere but the Black Dragon River, probably on military orders not to film on the boundary with the Soviet Union.

The PLA team made a spectacular short documentary, showing army men beating out the fire and relief supplies coming in, trying (not entirely successfully) to capture the black totality of destruction. The August First studio is one of the largest in China. It has fifteen hundred workers on the payroll, but even its resources were strained by Black Dragon.

It was this film, many sequences of which were shown on Chinese television, that made Black Beard a household figure throughout the country. With his illegal black stubble he immediately captured the public imagination.

The Black Dragon fire became a Chinese media event, the first of its kind. Before Deng Xiaoping the

Chinese regime had not given the press access to catastrophic events. They were non-happenings, never reported, spoken of only in whispers. Chinese reporters
didn't see much, and the few foreign newsmen in the
Mao days saw even less. When the great Tangshan
earthquake occurred in August 1976, just before Mao's
death, a very tight lid was placed on coverage, even
though this was the greatest earthquake in contemporary Chinese history and one of the world's worst.

Now came the world's greatest forest disaster and the
PLA's heroic efforts to end it. Never before had the PLA
played so important and dramatic a nonmilitary role. It
was, the PLA studio said, the worst disaster in the history of Communist China.

Foreign newsmen were not permitted to go to the
Heilongjiang area. Border regions are closed to foreign
correspondents. (My visit there was an exception.) But
there were no restrictions on the Chinese media.
China's newspapers, radio, and TV have become very
energetic in post-Mao times. Correspondents and television crews from all over the country descended on
Harbin, Shenyang, and Qiqihar and made their way by
train or plane north to the fire region.

At least 160 correspondents arrived in the Hinggan
area in the course of the fire. They were not met with
open arms. Some were picked up by the police, put
back on trains or planes, and sent out of the area.
Others found themselves detained for twenty-four
hours or longer by local officials. They could find no
rooms in the few hotels or lodging places, restaurants
would not serve them, they couldn't buy food, and
telephones were not available on which to call their

offices in Beijing or Shanghai. They made on-the-spot protests, their editors weighed in — nothing changed. Finally they published articles on the mistreatment in the press. To no avail.

The newsmen were doing what comes naturally to newsmen, but this was something new to China and particularly to the tight company of the forest world. The newsmen naturally felt they should get into the field, as close to operations as possible. They questioned officials, they interviewed fire victims, they found heroes and heroines, they wrote up the fire as best they could. Most of all they wrote about Black Beard. They printed his picture and put him on television. He got almost as much publicity as Chairman Mao did when he swam the Yangtse in July 1966 and kicked off the Cultural Revolution.

Another person to whom the press talked was a fourteen-year-old boy from Ma Lin, a young hero of the fire. When I saw Zhou Jinbao he still had an ugly burn scar at the corner of his right eye and another bad scar on the lower cheek of his round face. His man-sized hands were covered with burn tissue. I met him with his father at Tahe. He looked very adult in a pink sweatshirt and tan Eisenhower jacket with epaulets. He had been in one hospital or another ever since the fire.

Jinbao told his story easily, even dramatically. He showed me some of his clippings. Letters had come to him from all over the country. He had been on TV and was making speeches at some of the forest towns to tell the people of his experiences.

Jinbao said that he and his mother were asleep in

their house in Ma Lin on the evening of May 7. His father was nearby, on duty at the power station. Jinbao and his mother were awakened when a strong wind broke the north windows of their house. Startled by the crash, they looked out and saw the red sky and the advancing high flames coming down from the hills. Jinbao leapt out of bed.

"I pulled on my pants," he said, "but I could only get one leg in my trousers. I put on a T-shirt. My mother and I jumped from the window."

Jinbao talked in a high-pitched voice. There was much prompting by his father and other adults. He didn't need it. He was perfectly composed and had all the details at hand. That afternoon I had already interviewed a dozen people. He and his father had been waiting a long time.

Jinbao hadn't had a feeling of fear. Everything happened too fast. He heard their neighbors, a man of sixty-five and his son, next door. They were carrying buckets of water from the well, trying to save their house. He shouted to them to run. Then he rushed to a neighboring house where a nineteen-year-old mother lived with her four-month-old baby. He pounded on the window and roused her. Smoke was very thick, and the fire was almost upon them. He couldn't find the gate in the wooden fence that surrounded all their houses. Finally, he broke some slats and managed to get the young mother and her child, the old man, and his own mother through the fence. They found their way to the edge of the yard, where his mother slipped to the ground. She was ill and she couldn't go farther. He tried to get her to move, but she slumped to the ground, unconscious or dead. He waited to the last, then ran down the highway.

That was the last thing Jinbao remembered. The fire was upon them. People were running. He went blank. He awoke in water up to his chin. Some villagers had picked him up from the highway and put him in the river to save him from the fire.

All this time his father had been on duty at the power station. He dared not leave. The generator was the only source of power for the town. His family lived only a hundred yards away, but he could only hope they had made it to safety. Finally, once the fire passed by, leaping over the power station without harming it, he was able to leave. When he got out he found a truck on which Jinbao had been placed by the neighbors. "Mom didn't make it," the boy told his father. The truck took the boy off to Post 22 on the Gold Road and then to the big hospital at Jiagedaqi. The father said he'd stay in Ma Lin and see about his wife. The fire was so hot that it was 3:30 A.M. before he could make his way through the smoldering wreckage. His wife's body lay beside the roadway. "It looked like baked bread," he said.

As Jinbao listened to his father, he pursed his lips and ran the tip of his tongue over them again and again.

What did he want to do in life? I asked.

"I want to go to school and study hard and get a degree and then I'd like to become an expert on this forest. I love the forest. I love to hunt and pick berries."

Two days later he was leaving for Shanghai, where specialists hoped to wipe away the ugly scars of the fire with deft surgery.

X

Fauna and Flora

ONE FOGGY MORNING I drove out from Tahe, past the new elevator and flour mill that were being built not far from where the fire was halted, toward Xiu Feng. After an hour the fog lifted, and the countryside was bathed in sunshine. We stopped to get a better look at some of the scorched birches and larches and wandered in the cutover brush, picking *du shi*, a tart, bright red berry a little like a cranberry but smaller. There were yellow *mogu* mushrooms scattered on the forest floor. Mogu aren't tasty unless there is a small worm inside, my companion said. Actually, I didn't think they were so good with or without the worm, but perhaps that was because we were eating them raw. A bit farther on I spotted some beautiful *podsosni* (under-the-pines), as they are called in Russia. I don't know what they are called in Black Dragon country; I hadn't seen any of these mahogany mushrooms since I lived in Russia. I used to pick them in the pine forests just outside Moscow, and they were the best mushrooms I ever ate, even better than the morels of the Berkshire Hills.

It was a moment of peace and quiet, the echo of dragon winds and dragon fire long gone. I became truly aware of the quiet. There was not a sound to be heard and not a movement in the forest. It occurred to me that I had not seen a bird since I had entered the Hinggan Mountains. Of course, it was mid-September, but I did not think that all the birds would have gone south so early.

From then on I kept my eyes open. I saw no birds. I began to think of Rachel Carson's *Silent Spring.* The day before I left the forest I saw eight sparrows fly across the road from one clump of bushes to another. The absence of wildlife was so striking that I began to ask questions. The only other animals I had seen or heard were the stray dogs barking across the river at Ignashino, while I stood at Mohe looking over to the Soviet shore.

It was true. The wildlife was gone. No one could say for certain, but I did not find anyone in the Black Dragon country who remembered seeing a wild animal since the fire. Most people said that while there must have been considerable losses, the birds would surely come back, most of them, anyway. And some pointed out that the fire had come quite early, in May, and that in these northern mountains many birds had not yet entered the forest. If they had come during the fire, they probably would have halted on the Soviet side. Perhaps. I wondered if birds ever nested in burned trees or burned grass.

I remembered the Cloquet–Moose Lake fire when I

was a child in Minnesota. I had awakened one October morning to an owl staring blindly through my window from the lower branch of an old oak tree. Never had an owl appeared before in the heart of Minneapolis. The fire was 175 miles away, but the city was so shrouded in smoke that it was dusk at noontime. People reported seeing wolves and foxes, terrified and exhausted, limping down the center of streets. The toll of wildlife in the forest had been high.

I could not make a census of the Black Dragon land, but there was a good deal of evidence that the loss had been catastrophic. The toll in human terms had been comparatively low. The great fires in Cloquet–Moose Lake and, earlier, nearby Hinckley each had left several hundred dead. Black Dragon, by the official figures, had claimed just over two hundred. This was not merely good luck. The Chinese forest housed more inhabitants than the northern woods of Minnesota. The low human toll reflected skill in organization, protection, and evacuation.

But the wildlife? What evidence I could find was not promising. Wang Heping, the alert PLA political officer, had kept a diary of his thirty days in the wilderness, recording not one bird, not one living wild creature. The Hinggan Mountains are famous for moose. *Hanbi*, moose nose, is a delicacy served at banquets. Wang saw one dead moose. Only the antlers had survived the fire. Perhaps some had escaped by swimming to the Soviet banks of the Black Dragon River. But not many. I did not think that *hanbi* would soon again grace ceremonial tables.

The Hinggan Mountains were not the terrain of the

famous Siberian tiger, but the forest had been rich in black and brown bear. Not much chance that these lumbering creatures, fast as they could move in short dashes, had survived the hurricane of fire. Wang saw no bear, but he met a young soldier who had encountered a big one. The soldier had run for the nearest tree and managed to shinny up. To his amazement the bear ran off in fright, its balance obviously upset by the terror of the fire. Another soldier had a more familiar story. He awoke in his tent to find a bear putting its paw on his coat. The soldier grabbed for the coat, but the bear tore it out of his hand and ran away.

Wang saw four rabbits scorched and dead, victims of a fire they could not outrun. No birds. He looked in vain for *fei long*, the handsome Manchurian partridge, called the flying dragon. The tender meat is diced and served with its own sauce at special dinners. Three times in the forest I was served flying dragon; obviously, some had been put away in food lockers before the conflagration. But not one person had seen the magical creature since May 7.

Few of those I questioned showed much interest in birds or bears or moose. Human questions were on their minds. As for wild creatures, perhaps they had been wiped out, perhaps they hadn't. Time would tell.

I thought of the fires roaring over the land, one hundred feet high, moving at 30 miles an hour — what bird or beast would escape the holocaust? Yes, plant life with luck and years might regenerate. Wildlife? It depended on the Black Dragon River. Animals on the other side might cross over; birds might again nest in the ruins of the forest. But it would be a long time before the scarlet and gold of the flying dragon would light the dark corridors of the great sea of green.

The flame of the dragon bird is not to be found in serious studies of the Black Dragon Forest. And yet the forest was born in fire. No man knows whether it will die by fire, but a computer calculation would suggest that this is more likely than not. Fire is essential to forest life. In nature all forests burn from time to time, the fires set by nature — by lightning strikes for the most part — causing cyclical changes and new balances in forest and vegetative life. Historically, the change and rotation of animal, bird, fish, and insect life, of all life, in fact, are regulated by this savage, uncontrollable element — a catalyst of life and death, eternally progressing, eternally changing.

The great conifer mass of the Black Dragon country came into being at about the same time and under much the same circumstances that prevailed generally over the Eurasian and North American continents and, sometime after the Ice Age, gave rise to the forests that once covered Greenland, Iceland, Scandinavia, Russia, Siberia, China, Korea, Alaska, Canada, and the northern United States. Exactly when the Hinggan Forest first emerged Chinese naturalists cannot say for certain. They know that in the early Tang dynasty, eighth century, the province of Liaoning, lying just south of Black Dragon country and now barren of natural forests, was covered with forest, as was the Korean peninsula. Examination of Hinggan soils and rock structures suggests that as early as the third and fourth centuries of the last glacial period conifers spread through the area, as they did in so much of the northern hemisphere, replacing broadleaf trees. Earlier the region was probably grasslands, quite possibly swampy and not supportive of a forest.

The types of conifer varied from latitude to latitude and depended on elevation, climate, soil, water, and prevailing winds, the conditions that enhance or inhibit silviculture. In the extraordinary continental vastness of Siberia and China, the tree that rose to dominant position, for the most part, was *Larix dausica*, what the Chinese call Xianyan larch. This handsome tree resembles spruce and grows to between eighty and one hundred feet in the Greater and Lesser Hinggan forests and the Siberian forest north of the Black Dragon River. It is usually somewhat taller on the Chinese side because of the better soil and north-facing slope. The diameter may reach forty inches.

The *Larix dausica*, like all larch, is a member of the great pine family, and although a conifer, it is in botanical terms deciduous. The common type in the United States, the tamarack, turns a pleasant gold in autumn. So do some of the European and Chinese varieties. It is one of the finest of woods, highly valued for shipbuilding because of its resistance to salt water and exposure, widely used for poles and house construction, resinous and fragrant in oils.

There are ten to twelve principal kinds of larch, some found only in specific regions such as the Himalayas. For centuries, or perhaps millennia, it has been the primary wood of China.

Xu Youfang, deputy forestry minister and a specialist who has done seven years of academic forest studies, said it was difficult to determine to which generation today's Black Dragon Forest belongs. Conifers usually were succeeded by broadleafs, with mixed generations then preceding a new conifer era, not necessarily the same conifers that previously grew in the area.

"This depends on climate," he said. "Also, areas which had been swamp dry out. There is low vegetation, low temperatures, and the conifers appear. Then grasses develop, temperatures begin to rise, there is more moisture and birches take over. The birches and other deciduous growth spread more rapidly, then they burn and conifers may make a fresh start." The broadleaf species like higher temperatures and grow more rapidly.

He placed the age of the contemporary Hinggan Forest at 100 to 150 years. I thought that might be an underestimate. I had seen trees in Xilinji 100 and more years old. I had heard of a tree 150 years old that had literally exploded when hit by the hundred-foot wall of fire at Ma Lin.

I asked whether he thought the forest had burned more than 100 to 150 years ago. Yes, he said, but the forest might be older. Knowing the care with which the Chinese Empire kept chronicles of its dynasties, I was sure that had there been a devastating fire sweeping the Hinggan Range free of trees and giving the conifer a new start, there would be a notation in the annals, even though the Black Dragon region lay on an extremity of the empire. It was, after all, the heartland of the Manchu dynasty. I did not believe the Manchus would have left unnoticed a conflagration of such magnitude. And yet no such notation seemed to exist.

Fire, Minister Xu said, speeds regeneration and growth. In many cases fire explodes the hard seed pods and enables the conifer to regenerate in the newly carbonized soils. Fire clears the duff that sometimes lies so thick on the forest floor that seeds cannot germinate because they cannot reach the soil.

In the American south, the minister said he had heard, fire was often used to clear forest areas for regrowth and replanting. But he failed to add that this is not a recommended process. Nor do American forestry specialists look benignly on random and human-caused destruction of vast acreage of forests by fires.

But the minister stressed that fire was natural to the forest cycle; fire would stimulate conifer regrowth. There had been a very large fire near Tuqing in 1948, nearly thirty years before. Regrowth had been excellent. No, he conceded, it was not a conifer forest now. There was a lot of oak, scrub oak. Scrub oak, of course, is not a commercially useful tree. Lots of ash, aspen, birch, and other inferior trees could be expected now. But still — the minister kept trying to look to the bright side. It would take time, but in two hundred or three hundred years the forest, left to itself, should return to the rich conifer regime that had existed before May 6. This was the line Americans heard after the fire at Yellowstone.

The forestry specialists of China did not anticipate — as some of the political figures did — that the Black Dragon would, so to speak, regrow its tail. Zhou Zheng, chief forestry expert on the commission that investigated the fire, said yes, there will be regeneration. Prospects are not bad. But it will be birch and poplar.

He had examined burned-over areas. There was no doubt that the leading species in the first generation would not be conifers. He estimated the number of birch and poplar seedlings per hectare at 30,000, that of conifers at 1,000 to 2,000. The quick-growing broadleafs, outnumbering the conifers 30 to 1, would swamp the larch.

Past experience bore out the need for extreme conservatism in estimating regeneration of conifers. Zhao Guiyan, deputy director of the Tahe Forest Bureau, a man who was in the thick of the fire and who had spent years in both practical and scientific forest work, advised caution. Zhao, a rather pudgy man, chooses his words with care and often pauses to select the precise phrase to convey his meaning. He did not seem to make judgments lightly.

A forest cycle, he said, requires a minimum of twenty to thirty years. This first cycle in the Hinggan is not going to be coniferous. He pointed out that the greatest experience of fire they had had was to the south, in the Lesser Hinggan. There the regrowth is a mixture of broadleaf and conifer in which, as far as I could see, the broadleaf vastly predominates. Judging from more limited experience in the northern forest, he felt there should be some balance and hoped for "a fair number of conifers." That seemed reasonable to me.

"We can't be in too much of a hurry to effect a permanent regrowth of the forest. After all, the fire destroyed seven hundred and sixty thousand square miles of trees," Zhao said.

Of the dedication of Zhao Guiyan to the forest there could be no doubt. He described the forest and its products as "green gold." He saw the Hinggan as a national treasure to be maintained in perpetuity — no small task, he admitted, when you realize that the fire destroyed 14.4 million cubic yards of timber, a tremendous loss of an almost irreplaceable asset.

What none of the Chinese specialists liked to dwell on were the facts that between 1966 and 1981 nearly five million acres in the forests had burned and that 50 percent had been burned twice; or that fire was costing China 2.6 percent to 3 percent of her forest every year, not counting reburns. The loss due to the Black Dragon fire was equal to more than half of the fire losses in all of China since the founding of the People's Republic, in 1949.

At the time of the 1987 fire the Hinggan forests composed a bit more than one third of China's total timber reserves. In 1980 they had provided 30 percent to 40 percent of China's industrial lumber production. The Hinggan fire wiped out at least one third of China's principal reserve of first-class timber.

In the months after the Black Dragon fire China's leadership began to focus more and more on the reality of the forest's status. Gone was the easy talk of quick restoration. Now was the time for harsh statistics and bitter truths. The men who counted in Beijing saw that the situation was not going to be resolved by upbeat propaganda and punitive measures against Brush Cutter Wang. The removal of a handful of officials, local and national, was not going to restore the burned trees.

China was losing its forest resources at a rate of three million acres a year due to overcutting and fires. Gao Dazhan, the forestry minister who stepped in after the fire, estimated that in ten years the northeast and other main forests had lost 22.3 percent of their forest acreage and 28.6 percent of their forest resources to waste, fires, and overcutting. National consumption of forest resources amounted to 392 million cubic yards in 1985 against 270 million cubic yards of replacement.

The bulk of state spending in forestry had gone into cutting, only a pittance to maintenance. The state had put 1.6 billion yuan ($430 million) into Heilongjiang Province for timber cutting since 1964 against roughly 500 million yuan ($135 million) for management. Only half of this went for replacement planting.

The forestry industry, clearly, was organized on a production basis. Attention to forest practices and afforestation came second. In most cases, it was the responsibility of another set of officials. The forest farms, the line companies of the organization chart, were in the business of cutting trees at a profit. Their performance was considered the bottom line. There was a premium on holding costs down. They paid their workers well by Chinese standards, an average of 109 yuan a month and often 130 or 140 yuan a month. The workers got 20 percent to 30 percent premium pay for working in a hardship district. They received forest clothes, heavy clothing in winter, free housing, food subsidies. In many ways they lived better than if they had worked in Beijing.

The forest production companies — in fact, the timber industry as a whole — were rated on volume of production and margin of profit over costs. Since labor was their principal item of expense, they used labor to cut and process timber rather than engage in non-productive but essential tasks like building firebreaks, clearing the forest floor, replanting trees.

Thus, the forest bureaus, unless policed by management, tended to neglect tasks that did not bring in profit. This increased the danger of holocausts like the Black Dragon fire.

I was not reassured by changes that occurred in the year after the fire. The emphasis was still on production. Protective measures were undertaken, but slowly. The danger that the Black Dragon Forest would burn again was very much present.

To my mind the experience of the Lesser Hinggan Forest was the most frightening portent of what lay ahead for the Greater Hinggan. The Lesser Hinggan had been cut for decades. It had been savaged by the Japanese. It was notorious for fires. It had fulfilled the forester's prophecy — once burned, quickly burned again.

The Greater Hinggan had been almost free of fire. The fires that had struck it and the fires across the Black Dragon River on the Soviet side had — until 1987 — been like pennies cast into a great pool. They had made a dull ring and vanished from sight. Until the early 1970s there was no cutting in the Greater Hinggan, and there was still no cutting on the Soviet side. Fires there were usually caused by lightning. Strikes had been rather frequent because of the heavy ore deposits in the area, which attract lightning.

With the decision in 1972 to begin cutting in the Greater Hinggan, and with the pressures for profits and production that had accompanied Chinese economic expansion, the danger to the forest had multiplied.

What happened in May of 1987 almost certainly would happen again and again. Not always in such colossal proportions. But it would happen. The process of change was well established. The question now was, what would it bring?

XI

Consequences

NINTH REGIMENT COMMANDER Wang Aiwu
had sent a message at 9:00 P.M. on May 7 by military
wireless to Governor Hou Jie at Harbin that "deadly
fires" had broken out at Xilinji and Tuqing.

The message never reached the governor.

The governor is a big man of fifty-seven with a big
shock of black hair, which frequently falls over his
broad forehead. On the day he received me in his big
office in Harbin he was wearing a brown jacket and
dark blue trousers, with a cardigan over a striped shirt.
His shoes were black loafers, and his feet were very big,
at least size twelve. Everything about the governor
is big.

The governor travels a lot in China and abroad. His
province, Heilongjiang, has sister relationships with
Alaska and Wisconsin and what he called close connections with Minnesota. His open jacket displayed a
wide cowboy belt with a silver buckle decorated with a
single slash stroke. He looked a bit like a Texan, and I

guessed one of his sister governors had given him the western belt.

Governor Hou Jie is a booster and possesses a politician's hearty laugh. The Hinggan forests lie in his province. So do the great Daqin oil fields, where he often plays host to American and Canadian oilmen. He is proud of a Hong Kong–style hotel he had built for foreign visitors, complete with a small bellman wearing red pillbox cap and red jacket, the image of the little bellhop in the "Call for Philip Morris" commercials. He was pleased to hear I had stayed in his fancy hotel.

He spoke easily but a little apprehensively of the Black Dragon fire. He had not gotten the message from Commander Wang on May 7 because he happened to be in Los Angeles. His first news of the outbreak came when his interpreter picked up the *Los Angeles Times* and found a report that U.S. satellites had spotted a big fire in the Hinggan Forest, sixty miles long and twenty-five miles wide, causing serious losses. The governor called Harbin immediately (telephone connections to China from the United States are excellent). Harbin confirmed the news. He cut short his trip and rushed home.

He was able to catch a direct plane from Los Angeles to Tokyo within a few hours. He was too worried to think of anything else on the flight. The fire was a tragedy, and he knew his governorship was in jeopardy. To be in the United States when catastrophe hit his province would not play well in Beijing.

The governor sat in the first-class section with his interpreter back in tourist class. The only English words the governor knew were *yes, no, thank you,* and *good-*

bye. The stewardess asked if he would like dinner. He didn't understand what she was saying, so to be on the safe side he said no. A bit later she asked again, and he again shook his head. Finally she came back a third time, and this time he realized what the question must be and got something to eat.

It took ten hours to fly to Tokyo, and in that time the governor never stopped worrying. He liked the United States. He had visited it twice. He had made his first trip in 1976, going to sixteen states and inspecting American farm machinery. He had planned for this trip to be a long one, winding up in Alaska, but had hardly gotten started when news of the fire reached him.

He got back to Harbin exactly forty-eight hours after hearing of the Hinggan fire.

He was just in time. Vice Premier Li Peng (now premier) had come north to inspect the fire zone. The governor took part in the strategy and decision sessions that ultimately would bring the fire under control. This may have saved his political career. He offered his resignation, he said, and told the government that he would take responsibility for the disaster. With a laugh of relief, he added that the government had decided he wasn't to blame. Instead, the forestry minister lost his job. "I was Number Two," he said, "but next time a fire breaks out it will be my head."

The governor, I thought, was taking no chances. He was a hands-on executive, and this was emphasized by the arrangement of his office, on this bright September day, with the sun pouring in through big open windows behind our chairs. Great maps covered the walls, one of China and one of Heilongjiang Province. Across from us in the opposite corner, half screened by a divider next to which had been placed a coat tree, a washstand with a white enamel washbasin decorated with bright roses, and a towel hanging beside it, was a wooden bed covered by a blue and white spread. On it was a neat stack of blankets and pillows. A calendar hung on the divider, and beside it were a big desk with two telephones, one tan, one red, and two big cabinets for papers.

The message was clear. The governor was a twenty-four-hour executive, always on call, always ready to go to the scene of the crisis. At the moment of our interview his province was beset by floods. He had just spent two days directing reinforcement of the levees and was preparing to go off again as soon as we finished our talk.

The sun made patterns on the worn wall-to-wall red carpeting in the office. Whatever fear he had had for his career, the governor had regained his normal confidence. He was a self-made man who had come up through the ranks, a graduate in water control at the Harbin Institute (as was his wife), a former county executive and deputy governor. He had been governor since 1985.

He talked knowledgeably about the fire. It had quickly turned into a crown fire (the term is the same in Chinese as in English and means a fire burning in the treetops) and was driven by a wind as high as force 10, 60 miles an hour. No human being could control it. There had been, he said, about 400 casualties. The toll had recently been revised upward to 212 dead and 190 burned or injured. The most serious injury, he thought, was that of a man whose leg was amputated. There had been a loss of 850,000 cubic yards of cut timber and at least 40 million cubic yards of standing timber. He thought 15 million cubic feet of scorched timber could be salvaged if they got to it within five years (later estimates placed the salvage figure in considerable doubt). Just the week before, he had inspected the area with Vice Premiers Wang Li and Tian Jiyun, and they concluded that within seven to ten years the forest would be "restored." (Exactly how he defined that term was not clear.) He had inspected the fire zone in July and again in August. In July the forest was black and scorched. By August it had begun to green. Many people worried about long-term ecological effects. Not the governor. He didn't believe there would be serious consequences. In ten years the forest would be re-stored. Possibly there would be change in some limited areas. But he did not share fears that Beijing's weather would be affected.

The governor was determined to restore the forest. Replanting was already under way. The State Council had moved very rapidly.

He didn't think it would have made any difference if the Forest Service people had gotten earlier notice that large fires had broken out on the Soviet side of the Black Dragon. On the other hand, they should have been aware of the fires. If they hadn't known — they should have. He was very strong in placing blame on the forestry apparatus right down to the local level. It was true that you could not at first see the Soviet fires from the riverbank because of the elevation of the land. But the local people should have known. The border guards might have picked up some information, and the forestry people should have been alert to get information from them.

Two days after the governor got back to Harbin he had received a telephone call from his friend Governor William Sheffield of Alaska, who was concerned about the fire. Sheffield had told him that forest fires had broken out in Alaska just three days after the Chinese fire. Governor Hou Jie shared the feeling of many Chinese that there must have been some connection between the outbreak of the Black Dragon fire and blazes in other parts of the world at the same time.

In the aftermath of the fire, Beijing had given the governor more responsibility over the forest area. He was in overall control now of the Heilongjiang forest region, and if a new fire broke out, he would be held to account, no question about that. But he had no intention of permitting such a thing. All sorts of measures were being taken: new communications, new advanced equipment, more watchtowers, and many more rangers and forest police. Heads might roll but not, he hoped, his own.

I never got to see the infamous Brush Cutter Wang. A great number of people told me about his role in starting the fire, and he was denounced, especially by such high officials as Governor Hou Jie. Many others gave me sermons on the poor discipline of low-ranking workers.

Finally, after more than a year of investigation and an examination of seventeen hundred pieces of evidence, eleven men were put on trial in June 1988 in connection with the fire — seven officials and four workers. Wang was the only one whose picture was published on newspaper front pages, showing him impassive in the courtroom, flanked by PLA soldiers, seated within a little wooden-barred cage, his hands manacled. He got a sentence of six years and six months. Most Chinese thought this rather lenient.

I had no doubt of Wang's misdeeds nor of the poor discipline in the forest zone. This was brought out in the trial, and it clearly was matched by scandalous misconduct by some higher forestry officials.

On the eve of the trials a Beijing reporter went back to the Black Dragon Forest to write an article about new precautions being taken to prevent fires. One day, as he was ascending a rough mountain road in his jeep, he was astonished to encounter a Japanese luxury car, a Toyota Bluebird, struggling to make the rocky, steep climb, its shiny exterior splashed with mud. In another part of the forest he encountered heavy Chinese-made luxury cars, Red Flag limousines, carrying forest officials through the burned-over countryside. Astonished, he dug into the situation.

The reporter checked with the Hinggan prefecture and found that the government had advanced special funds to forest and county bureaus to replace trucks and jeeps destroyed in the fire. A quick audit showed that 121 cars had been bought illegally at a cost of more than 3 million yuan (about $1 million). The Tuqing Forest Bureau, which had been wiped out by the fire, bought at least one Red Flag limousine and some deluxe Soviet Volgas. Xilinji bought twelve cars illegally, and Amur — left a smoking ruin by the disaster —

bought nine new luxury cars for its officials. The reporter talked to an ordinary lower-level official who said, "After the disaster everything needs money. So money should be put to the best use, instead of buying luxury cars. When will there be a stop to this kind of conduct?"

The Black Dragon trial revealed that criminal negligence was not confined to brush cutters. Zhuang Xueyi, director of the Tuqing Forest Bureau, saved himself but did nothing to evacuate the Yuying forest farm. He escaped, leaving no one in charge. People did not know what to do. No one was evacuated, no one was mobilized to fight the fire. In the end 43 people were killed and 19 injured. That was almost half the toll of 103 burned to death in Tuqing.

Some of the officials at Xilinji were equally irresponsible. Li Yongqing, deputy party secretary of Mohe County, was charged with having leapt into his car, picked up his family, and raced out of the fire zone to safety, leaving the forest to burn and people to perish.

Qin Baoshan, Mohe County fire chief, was charged with sending four fire engines to save his own house at a time when Xilinji was burning end to end. He saved his house. The town was destroyed. He got four years in prison. Li Yi, who hired Brush Cutter Wang, got five years.

Several officials in Amur, where sixty people died, were convicted of fleeing the scene, commandeering cars or motorbikes. The head of the Yi Li Forest Bureau, Bao Guorong, ran off in a car with his wife, leaving a thousand people behind. Three of them burned to death.

Other reports deepened my feeling that Wang's role in the fire had been exaggerated. My curiosity was aroused when I learned that a second brush cutter, a man named Guo Yongwu, was convicted. He drew a three-year term. He worked at the Yixi farm in the Amur complex. His brigade leader got a two-year sentence for negligence. He didn't even know how to operate a brush cutter and had let Guo Yongwu employ a cutter without a safety catch.

The workers who were convicted all seemed to be itinerants. They drew sentences of 7, 6½, 5, and 3 years. The officials got 3 years each, except for one who got 4 years and another who got only 2.

I thought there were several peculiarities about those punished. Mechanical brush cutters had been used in the forest for many years. Hundreds of them were employed. No one, so far as I could ascertain, had ever complained about them as a cause or potential cause of fire. Like the thousands of chainsaws, winches, donkey engines, hoists, and other gasoline-powered forest gear, they were prized by forest management. They were efficient and they cut labor costs. The woods were dotted with depots storing gasoline to power this equipment. So far as I could learn, brush cutters had not been a fire hazard before the Black Dragon catastrophe, nor were any fires attributed to brush cutters in the period after the great fire. The Black Dragon, like any modern, commercially operated forest, required lots of gasoline-powered machinery. On the day of the great fire two brush cutters happened to be involved in two fires. Coincidence? Perhaps. Both guilty brush cutters happened to be itinerants. Coincidence? Perhaps.

Brush cutting is a job done in the United States and Canada by casual labor. In China, however, it falls into the skilled category.

Three forestry workers had been arrested on charges that they had started fires by careless smoking. Two of these men were charged with causing the Hu Wan fire, near Gulian. The third was picked up at the Xi Nan forest farm.

Three teenagers were arrested near Tahe. They had gone swimming and built a fire to dry their clothes. The fire got into the undergrowth and spread to the forest. The oldest boy was held on charges, while the two others were let off with a reprimand.

I wondered about those cigarette smokers. Smoking was not forbidden. Cigarettes and tobacco were sold freely in the forest area. Matches, however, were not sold. I asked if there had been any reduction in smoking since the fire. No one thought there had been. There were rules about smoking, as there were about camp-fires and brush cutters. Had there been a breakdown in discipline just lately, as suggested by some of the higher-ups? I could not judge on the basis of my brief observation. But I did notice that jeep drivers, truck drivers, and most of the forest officials I talked to smoked a lot. I did not see anyone carelessly throw away a cigarette, but such smoking seemed to me a constant hazard.

I asked Commander Ge Xueling, vice director of Jiagedaqi's Fire Control Center, about Smokey Bear. He smiled. He had become very fond of Smokey Bear in his travels in Canada. Did they have a Smokey Bear in the forest? No, he said; he wished they did. I kept an eye out for warnings about smoking. There must have been many, but the only ones I saw were posted outside a dining hall in Mohe.

At a higher level the forestry minister had been dismissed; so had the deputy minister in charge of fire prevention (regarded by many with whom I talked as a first-class man). Three other persons in the ministry had been disciplined. One got a warning and another had to make a self-criticism, but none of this went into the permanent files.

As for the field level, twenty-three lost their jobs, including the head of the prefecture in Jiagedaqi (in charge of both Tahe and Mohe counties), the chief of the Tahe Forest Bureau (also known as an able man), the Mohe County leader, Mrs. Wang, and an assortment of other forest farm, forest bureau, and county officials. I had been told that the most serious case was that of Gao Boxing, the Tahe County leader. It had been turned over to the procurator for investigation of criminal responsibility, but Gao's name did not figure in the trial of June 1988. The procurator did not bring charges. However, Gao was dismissed as secretary and expelled from the Communist party. What underlay this apparently random punishment was hard to say. To an outsider it seemed to follow a conventional bureaucratic pattern. Disaster struck, and the "usual suspects" were rounded up and punished, even though the true causes were wind and weather. Had the field near Gulian been as waterlogged on May 6 as it was when I saw it in September, nothing would have come of Wang's sloppiness. The same was true for the cigarette smokers.

I could not believe that the usual suspects had done anything that had not been done thousands of times before in the forest.

As for the officials, instinct suggested that a disaster is always a good time to pay off old scores. *Someone* has to take the blame. Governor Hou Jie was lucky; the forestry minister got fired. Commander Ge was lucky; he was passed over and the deputy minister in charge of fire prevention got the black spot. Why had the hero of Xilinji, Mrs. Wang, been removed? That dismissal, I suspected, might well have had its roots in her origins, in a perception of her as an outsider. She was a brave and principled woman, but she was not quite a member of the inner circle.

I don't know who selected those to be disciplined, but I do know bureaucracy and I assume there was a formula — somebody who said "I'll keep one of mine, you keep one of yours." That is what happens in American bureaucracies. Chinese bureaucracies are not much different.

And there is something else — the "iron rice bowl."

The iron rice bowl is usually spoken of as a Chinese concept, one established by the revolution. Once you join an organization you have lifetime tenure; you cannot lose your job; you never again need fear the starvation and poverty in which Chinese peasants and proletariat lived before the People's Republic. The concept — it is one of the targets of the reforms of Deng Xiaoping and Zhao Ziyang — has many permutations. It carries a little of the aroma of the old Chinese clan, in which everyone in the clan looks out for each other and outsiders are outsiders. This philosophy can take extreme forms. If a Chinese truck breaks down on the highway, the driver stands by and waits, often for days, for a truck from *his* company to come along and help. Drivers from other companies whiz right by, just as the man whose truck is stalled whizzes by when they are stuck.

The forest community is one big family. It came into being at the beginning of the seventies. It was like a separate kingdom inside the remote Hinggan forests. There was nothing else there. You worked for the forest; that was it. The jobs were good. Not many outsiders applied, nor were they encouraged. There were several categories of employment. The permanent staff was the elite, and it included the bureaucrats, the engineers, and the group and crew leaders of the loggers and timbermen. Once in, never out. They were there for life. It was *their* rice bowl, and no one was going to take it away. Their relationship to Beijing was to the Forestry Ministry; an umbilical cord, never broken, connected them. Their job in the Black Dragon Forest was to cut timber and ship it, to make money for the state, and to live what was, in Chinese terms, an agreeable life without much interference.

The forest had created a durable hierarchy and structure. Beneath the category of permanent staff — just as well paid and treated — were contract workers. They signed up for five-year periods in the forest and were indistinguishable from staff. Their jobs, and there were many, were reserved exclusively for relatives of staff:

sons, daughters, aunts, uncles, cousins, or very close friends. No one else need apply. In fact, no one else would be hired.

When I expressed amazement at this nepotism the forest people looked back in equal amazement. "Doesn't anyone complain?" I asked. No one, they insisted. The system ensured that they had a high-quality, stable body of personnel. It bulwarked the family and made certain that no one worked in the forest who did not live there, had not grown up there, did not know and understand the forest. It was a great source of strength. The only fear was that some young people would move out of the forest and go to the big cities. That was a serious threat.

Below the two elites was the third category, into which fell so many of those charged with wrongdoing in the catastrophe — the transient labor force. This force, ever-shifting, varying in numbers according to the time of year, was paid on a piecework basis, somewhat less than the permanent and contract forces and without the perks provided the elite.

About one fourth of the workers were contract labor; the itinerant constituent probably was 10 percent. The forest, it seemed to me, had created a band of brothers. Scapegoats had to be found for the great fire. They would be picked with exquisite care. The one big family with its iron rice bowl would survive, even if the Black Dragon did not.

Among those whom I came to think of as good company men I did not hear much talk about the broader issues. The question of the survival of the Black Dragon Forest as an eternally renewing treasure of China's society and economy didn't touch them. There seemed to be no real interest in ecological or broad human considerations. These were line men. First had come the *Sturm und Drang* of the fire itself, then came the political controversy.

Perhaps it was unfair, but I thought of a story told me by Liang Tingyi, an information officer of PLA Unit 81156 who had gotten to the fire zone from Harbin on May 10. Liang Tingyi was a very young, tremendously enthusiastic officer, a captain, I believe (he wore no insignia of rank), and he told me how a PLA commander had saved the lives of forty children and some old people trapped by the advancing flames in Xilinji. The officer ordered them to dig little pits, deep enough so that only their noses protruded from the moist sand. They lay down head-to-head; that way, if sparks set fire to their clothing, they could help each other put them out. The fire passed them over. Yes, a few were scorched, but most of them came through untouched.

In a manner of speaking, I thought, that was how the forestry's band of brothers had passed through the political firestorm.

So far as I could see, the government had done an excellent job in building new housing for the forest workers and making good the losses of their worldly goods.

The streets of Xilinji, Ma Lin, Tuqing, and the rest resounded with the sound of hammers and saws. Xilinji had thirty-eight construction companies from almost as many cities, from places as distant as Gansu, putting up new buildings. The housing was superior to what had burned — brick and cement construction, two- and three-room apartments, kitchens and interior bathrooms, gas stoves, piped water, central heating, a TV aerial on every house, new stores, sidewalks, and asphalt streets. A big step forward from the raw timber towns that burned down.

No other Chinese disaster had met with such prompt and generous government action. Four years after the great Tangshan earthquake people were still squatting in temporary shelters. By October 15, 1987, all but 10 percent of the fire victims had their own homes — better houses than they had ever had. Concern for the fire victims had been shown from the first day. On May 8 six planes dropped food and medical supplies in the Ninth Regiment compound for the citizens of Xilinji.

The fire left 33,706 homeless. Each person without a home was given — on two separate occasions — 71 yuan in relief funds as well as food and clothing. Some 600,000 items of clothing were sent to the fire victims: 28,477 quilts, 22,000 mattresses, a blanket for each household, and 10,000 sets of bedclothes.

The record of Xilinji was a good example. Of the 5,193 households there on May 6, 1987, a total of 3,643 were destroyed. Of Xilinji's 22,221 residents, 19,458 were affected in one way or another. More than 25,000 square yards of housing were burned. So were 262 items of machinery (cars, trucks, et cetera) and 2 million pounds of grain and flour. In the town 190,000 cubic yards of timber were burned, and there was an economic loss to the town of 120 million yuan, or about $40 million, exclusive of personal losses and losses to the forest industry.

By October 1987, a total of 170,000 square yards of housing had been built, of which nearly 130,000 were for personal use. By October 15, 1987, all but about four hundred households had been resettled in new housing. The remainder doubled up over the winter and got their new houses by June 15, 1988.

It would be difficult to match this record for bureaucratic speed. A special State Council group had been sent into the fire zone on June 2, 1987, to assess needs. It reported that 600,000 yards of new floor space were needed. Within five days a standard design for the housing project was sent to the State Council, which approved it two days later. The plan called for building 500,000 square yards by the end of 1987. In fact, 400,000 were completed before year's end.

All of the new housing, Governor Hou Jie told me, would be fireproof.

With all its expectable flaws, the job done in fighting the great Black Dragon fire and caring for its victims was one of which China could be proud. The State Council had moved in quickly and decisively. The PLA had done well, overall, and the rehabilitation program was better than those provided by any former Chinese government. In contrast, for instance, with the reactions to the Armenian earthquake of 1988 and the Tangshan earthquake of 1976, the emergency performance of both the government and the PLA was outstanding. But the long-range consequences presented a different and more difficult question.

XII

The Wasteland

COMMANDER Ge Xueling sat across from me beside a window in the roomy Soviet-made MiG-8 helicopter. On the table between us was a map of the Black Dragon Forest on which he had crosshatched the area of the fire.

The cross-hatching began west of Xilinji at the Inner Mongolian border and sprawled east to and beyond Tahe. The hatching reached the Black Dragon River for a distance greater than I had been told, beginning not far from the old Russian *ostrog* at Albazin and skirting the river for possibly seventy-five miles. The southern boundary formed a long, slow curve paralleling the railroad. On Commander Ge's chart the fire's outline looked like a human brain outlined in soft graphite.

I had talked to scores of people about the fire, and now I wanted to bring the picture into focus by flying over it with the man who knew this haunted realm better than any other. The Hinggan Forest was Ge's world. No one else understood so well the meaning of the fire that to me had begun to possess an almost mystical quality, representing a symbol, which I did not entirely understand, of the direction of our future.

We waited for a moment or two on the improvised helicopter pad, saying good-bye to those who had helped me to gather impressions and data on the fire and the forest. Then the noisy machine lifted off a bit unsteadily and rose over Xilinji, the sprawl of the fire visible in the black ruins and new construction.

I knew that Ge lived in a state of apprehension. The forest crisis was far from over. For him it was just beginning. The virgin woodland that he had so loved was no more, and the peril of fire had not lessened. It had been increased by the 1987 fire, and he would stand in the shadow of future fires the rest of his life.

He — and I — were disturbed by what we knew of the possible ecological effects of the fire. No one understood yet what the consequences would be. Yes, the commander had said, he believed the forest could regenerate. But not in his lifetime would he see a new conifer forest. Yes, they would plant and plant, but he was a practical forest man; he knew the next generation of trees would not be conifers. Nor the next after that. When would the forest return to conifers? Like the Canadian forest experts, he knew that this would take luck. A century? Two centuries? Or would the Hinggan follow the path of some great Chinese forests into the eternal hell of desert sand?

The forest bequeathed to me a sense of deep foreboding. I felt I was participating in an inquest on the fate of the earth. I was a little (I thought) like a Lilliputian stumbling on the lifeless bulk of Gulliver clumped in a tangle of weeds that seemed like towering conifers.

The haunt of the forest, I realized, had entered my bones; it was a kind of sorcery, a Manchurian Birnam wood. Never had a story so affected me.

Commander Ge was tapping my wrist for attention and pointing to the window. We were approaching Tuqing, or the dark spot where Tuqing once stood. He leaned close to my ear, and his shout came to me as a whisper over the noise of the copter; "Burned. All burned." He sat back in his seat, his face Indian pipestone, staring at the window, checking his map, making tiny corrections with the sharp point of his pencil.

I could see far to the north the vague outline of the Black Dragon, the black ruin extending across the landscape. I could not see whether it touched the riverbank as did Ge's chart or halted just short of the bank. It did not, I realized, make any difference. A mile or two, a few hundred yards in the raven sea.

I began to understand why the burned-down forest had left such despondency in my heart. It was not the timber, not the loss of cash-and-carry, not the destruction of the grubby forest towns or the loss of forest machinery so carefully itemized in the balance sheets of the forest accountants: the tractors, the bulldozers, the trucks, the backhoes. I knew their value to China, which had invested millions to bring to her use this treasure of timber.

It was not even the death of innocent people that so

moved me. It was the totality of it all — as if in frantic rage at invasion of his forest kingdom, the Black Dragon had turned on those whom it was his duty to guard and, with a gust of fiery breath, wiped it all out: men, women, children, animals, birds, trees.

I understood how fanciful my concept was. This was not the precise language of engineers, the earthy constructs of professional foresters, or the jargon of clerks. I understood that emotion had swept away the traditional objectivity of a reporter.

I sorrowed for the people and their losses, but what so moved me was the eternity of what had happened. The lives would never be lived again. The forest was gone. There would be other people and other forests, but not these. We had not really begun to study the consequences. China's State Council had set up a commission to examine the ecological effects. I knew what it would say. No permanent ecological damage. No permanent change in the climate. The forest would regrow, but in a different configuration. No permanent increase in erosion. Beijing's climate would not change. The deserts would not expand. The report would be upbeat, forward-looking.

But the people of the forest knew that changes would come. They were already coming, *and they would be forever.* The airy estimates of the bureaucrats, as it turned out, would be deflated by both the immensity of the disaster and political intransigence. The dark words that Commander Ge had spoken to me as we boarded the helicopter — "The danger is not over!" — would reverberate in Beijing and elsewhere in the nation. The danger had not passed. China had acquired a new companion. The dragon of fire would live beside her for decades.

I had thought during the days when I walked through the carbonized woods at Xilinji and Ma Lin and Amur that I was following the trail of a forest that had died, walking step-by-step across the black skeleton, a march of death in the world's greatest forest.

Now I looked down on that black skeleton. I could see tens of miles in all directions. There were few clouds in the sky. Ge stared at the expanse. From time to time he grasped my wrist and whispered "All burned." A minute later he would do it again, point to the ground and say: "All burned."

Out the window the ground lay like a shadow from the moon burned into the body of the Green Sea, the forest that had started in fire and, I feared, would die in fire. Once it got dry enough, once the wind blew strong, somewhere in that expanse there would be a spark. One spark. As Mao Zedong was fond of saying, "One spark can start a prairie fire." It did not take more to raise a conflagration that a man on the moon could have seen.

Suddenly I realized that Commander Ge was not merely gazing at the ground, checking the points of the flight. His eyes were grim and roving. He was an Indian scout on a high ridge, his vision ranging over the landscape for the enemy. The commander's enemy was fire. There had been two small fires during the summer — nothing serious — but now everything was serious. We were at the opening of the fall period of peril.

The presence of the helicopter was a signal of that peril. Not until September 15, formal start of the high-risk period, was the copter released to the Forest Service for fire patrol. The Forest Service rented its copters and planes through the Civil Aviation Administration of China, China's civil air service, at exorbitant rates (2,500 yuan an hour) and under ridiculous conditions. The CAAC required a crew of four to six, did not permit the copter to fly in winds of more than 20 miles an hour, did not permit a takeoff if the flight would delay the crew's lunch, did not permit the copter to park in a field overnight. Like many a business, it put profit before public duty. The fire could wait; the CAAC men had to have their lunch.

Commander Ge was looking for fires, and he could hardly take his eyes from the forest and broken country that opened below us. I watched, too. I caught my breath when I saw in the distance what looked like a column of smoke. Then another. I pointed them out to the commander. "Showers," he said. "Good." They were on the line of the Hinggan Mountains, the ridge where their gradual descent to the Black Dragon River begins.

In the cabin lolled three or four crew members in their brown leather jackets. The plane had been fitted for VIPs, red carpet on the floor, five aluminum folding chairs with red vinyl seats, a counter but no liquor. The spare crewmen were bored. One dozed, two read what looked like Chinese paperbacks. Not a glance at the devastation below. They had seen it all, had flown through the fire and smoke of May 1987. They reminded me of World War II bomber crews transferred to peaceful missions of the Air Transport Service.

Commander Ge had crosshatched his map in three shades — the worst burn, the medium burn, and the light burn. So much of it was heavy burn. The more I looked out the window, the larger it seemed to grow.

We flew as the wind had flown on the night of May 7, west to east, and were beginning a gentle turn south toward Jiagedaqi. The forest was no longer solid black. It was a patchwork, regions of golden silk, great swatches of black velvet, and squares of tousled green, stitched together by power lines, roads, and the rail-road. I could see the bright flags of the aspens, and I thought there was something sinister about them — as if they could not wait to take over.

I turned to Commander Ge and told him, shouting into his ear, "This makes me very sad." He tried to smile and said: "Bad."

We did not exchange much more than twenty words on the flight. No need. We knew what each felt. At 4:00 P.M. we landed at Jiagedaqi. The helicopter sank straight down, and a cloud of chaff and paper scraps were flung up into the slanting afternoon sun as high as the wall of flames at Xilinji. Ge and I smiled at each other. We were thinking the same thought.

We ambled off the copter and over to the terminal. I looked away for a moment, and Ge had gone. Vanished. He was leaving me here. We had not said good-bye.

I lay awake half the night at Jiagedaqi. I could not get the image of the dead forest out of my mind. It was, I thought, like the death of a continent. Nor could I forget the sadness of Commander Ge.

When I got back to Beijing I went over my impressions. Perhaps I had been too emotional. I knew I had never been so moved by a story, not even in the blitz of London or Leningrad after the siege.

Perhaps I had overreacted. Possibly the forest would not burn and reburn ad infinitum. The larch does have great powers of resistance. It grows very thickly and deposits no duff on the forest floor. In a compact forest it defends itself very well against fire. Maybe the fire had not done as much damage as originally estimated. Maybe many trees had been so lightly touched they would not die. After all, the wind had been so strong that the flames raced through the crown in great leaps, leaving large untouched swatches, a "flying fire," as the Chinese liked to say.

There was another positive factor. Gradually improving relations with the Soviet Union under Mikhail Gorbachev's policy of *glasnost* might make cooperation between the Chinese and Soviet forest administrations more likely.

An important harbinger of such cooperation was seen in August 1988, when Chinese and Soviet delegations reached an agreement for Chinese timbering teams to enter the burned-out Soviet forests east of Chita and cut and process timber scorched in the fire on the Soviet side of the Black Dragon River. The Chinese logging teams were attached to the Inner Mongolian segment of the Hinggan Forest, west of the area of the Black Dragon fire.

Had China received a warning from the Russians of the great fires that had started in Soviet forests as much as two weeks ahead of theirs, the Chinese forests could have been put on a high alert. Yet, as the Canadians conceded, no one, Chinese or non-Chinese, could have predicted such a fire. It was, all agreed, bigger than one could have imagined. No one had seen nor heard of such a thing.

It was the worst fire of our times, the worst fire (if the Chinese and Soviet fires are taken together) in three hundred years or maybe more. So the Canadians thought. I was reminded of Black Beard's words — the human body could not live without its heart; a forest could not live without its heart. Perhaps my feeling of apprehension was not so unrealistic after all.

XIII

The Future

WHEN I BEGAN talking to American forest specialists about the Black Dragon fire, I quickly found that none had any information. They had heard that it was a very big fire. That was all.

As I described the dimensions of the great fire, the precedent that they immediately called to mind was that of the Cloquet–Moose Lake fire, in Minnesota, of October 12, 1918. That was the biggest fire any had heard of. It had burned a million acres in one day, mostly after 2:00 P.M.

I knew a good deal about this fire. My father was in a National Guard outfit that was rushed to the north in the emergency. I remembered the fire, the stories my father had told, and the smoke that hung over Minneapolis for days.

Nearly four hundred people lost their lives, almost all on that one day. One of the tasks of my father and his men was to remove charred bodies from the burned-out farms and cabins and stack them, as he said, like cordwood at the stations of the Great Northern Railroad.

The fire had struck in newly logged timber country, an area that had been cut over a year before with little care. The wind that day had been recorded at 60 miles an hour at nearby Duluth (some estimates put the speed at 70 miles an hour), a hurricane force that drove the flames over the broken forest with unparalleled rapidity. The fire burned over and destroyed two thousand square miles of forestland, mostly in the afternoon and evening of October 12.

The characteristics of the Cloquet–Moose Lake fire resembled those of the Black Dragon in uncanny detail. In both cases the extraordinary force of the wind — force 10 or 11 on the Beaufort scale — was coupled with extreme dryness. The Minnesota forest had been cut over; the Chinese fire began in areas where there had been, for the most part, recent cuttings. As in Minnesota, fires had broken out in China in four or five places almost simultaneously. If the American fire offered a pattern for the future of the Black Dragon Forest, the omens were not good. Cloquet–Moose Lake never regenerated, never recovered. To this day it is a tumble of second-rate trees, burned and reburned.

On the subject of regeneration, the American specialists largely echoed opinions of their Chinese colleagues. The first generation of the Black Dragon would be broadleaf, not larch. Future generations depended on two factors — how high a percentage of larch seedlings was mixed with the faster-growing aspen and birch, and whether there was a new fire. The repeat fire held the key. A repeat fire or a series of repeats would doom the chances for early regeneration of the great Green Sea of larch. It was not realistic to expect a dominant larch generation for at least a hundred years. "Quickie" talk would only lead to false expectations.

Dr. David Smith of the Yale Forestry School said that, barring more fires and allowing enough time, "the aspen and birch will tire and the larch will begin to prevail." He believed there would be a minimum of sixty to seventy years of deciduous prevalence — if, again, there was no new fire.

There have never been larch forests such as those of the Black Dragon in the Western Hemisphere. The only large larch stands in America today are in Montana, and they do not begin to match the grandiose scale of the Chinese-Soviet forest.

If as many as one hundred larch per acre spring up in a hundred years, undisturbed by fire, there should be a new larch forest, Smith felt. "Then you could have wall-to-wall larches" was the way he put it.

What puzzled the American specialists most was how the extraordinary larch forest had come into being. So great a stand of roughly equivalent age could only have risen in the wake of a great catastrophe, the burning over of the vast area at one time, possibly 150 or 200 years ago in a conflagration that would dwarf even that of May 1987. None had heard of such a fire (nor had the Chinese).

Myron L. Heinselman, the leading specialist on the Boundary Waters forest, which lies on the Minnesota-Ontario border, has devised techniques for dating the age and size of forests and of past major fires. By careful analysis of burn marks, scars, growth patterns, and other clues he can determine when a forest was born and how. These techniques have not yet been applied to the Black Dragon Forest, but both Chinese and American specialists believe it was born after a continental holocaust, fulfilling the classic forest syndrome — birth by fire, death by fire.

Larch is not tolerant of shade. Larch grows very well after a fire that destroys surrounding vegetation, and it thrives in fire ash. This is the most hopeful characteristic for strong regeneration of the larch forest.

But the fact is, no one has had any experience with so large an area of devastation. The North American experts are familiar with the aftermath of fires of 100,000 acres or even 500,000 acres, but nothing like the 3 million Chinese acres and the 15 million Soviet acres of the Black Dragon. In 1985 there was a very large fire in Canada's Northwest Territories, destroying possibly a million acres. But this did not burn a mature forest. It raged over masses of jack pine, tundra, scrub oak, and other inferior species. And even the Yellowstone fire of summer 1988 burned over a much smaller area, in comparison — 1.2 million acres, of which as little as one tenth was estimated to have been destroyed.

So much of the Black Dragon's future depends on whether it burns again and reburns and reburns. When this happens a few times, any hope of regeneration vanishes, and even the prospect of replanting becomes dim.

The picture of the fire and the forest on the Soviet side of the Black Dragon River is still blurred. Moscow has issued no report of any content on the vast fires that blazed over millions of Siberian acres at the same moment that the Black Dragon Forest, to the south, was being consumed. There were a few perfunctory reports in the local Siberian newspapers but nothing in *Pravda* or *Izvestiya*. For the most part that seems to reflect the prevailing atmosphere in Siberia. Vast amounts of acreage burn every year. They are too distant to attract much attention. A few years ago I flew over eastern Siberia from Khabarovsk, in the Soviet Union, near where the Black Dragon River branches off from the Chinese-Soviet border and enters Russia as the Amur River. For an hour or two, or so it seemed to me, I was never out of sight of a forest fire. They seemed to be blazing over thousands, possibly tens of thousands, of acres, sending huge pillars of flame and smoke in the air. So far as I could observe not a human being was paying any heed.

Inattention to East Siberian forest fires is, in fact, widely prevalent. As a Soviet forestry specialist pointed out, these forests will not be used commercially for at least one hundred years. To be certain, they contain valuable timber: larch, pine, spruce. But if the forests do not burn, they will deteriorate and fall prey to age and disease. In the long run, better let them burn and trust that by the time the timber is needed, new larch stands, healthy and vigorous, will have sprung up.

Siberia has been the scene of many forest catastrophes. When the great Tunguska meteorite struck on June 30, 1908, with an explosion heard six hundred or seven hundred miles away, it set off an enormous blaze that raged over hundreds of square miles of North Central Siberia. Early in World War I the great forest fire of 1915 blazed over a third of Siberia in a narrow path from somewhere west of Lake Baikal almost to the Urals. The Soviet fires of spring 1987 were big, no doubt of that. But no one in the Siberian forest service — possessed of excellent fire-fighting equipment, trained forest rangers, smoke jumpers, scooper planes, and all the modern techniques — thought of combating them on a national scale. Enough to protect isolated towns and villages. As for the rest — let it burn. In a hundred years the timber will be all the better.

No other country in the world can afford that rationale. Not even Russia is likely to be able to live with this philosophy much longer. If there are going to be more fires alongside either bank of the Black Dragon River, mutual concern and common sense will inevitably drive the Chinese and the Russians back into cooperation to save this priceless heritage.

Those who have seen the satellite photos of the 1987 fire report that the Chinese and Russian fires burned almost in tandem along the river. Contrary to the protestations of many Chinese authorities, the fires on both sides of the river burned to the edge, and in at least one instance, in a locality northeast of Mohe, the fires blazed simultaneously only a few hundred yards apart. It may well be true, as the Chinese insist, that no Russian sparks landed on Chinese trees, but if so that was sheer luck. When winds of 60 miles an hour are blowing it is not much of a trick for a shower of sparks to fly across a few hundred yards of water (or much less, in the case of the Ergun River, to the west of Heilongjiang Province).

After all, the specialists calculate that only about 20 percent of the Black Dragon fire was on the Chinese side, while 80 percent of the burn was Russian, just short of the thirty thousand square miles of Scotland and fifteen times the size of the great Cloquet–Moose Lake fire.

If China finds herself better prepared to meet a vast fire emergency next time, the credit in so small measure may go to Horst Wagner, the German forestry specialist who is the chief expert for the World Bank.

Wagner has been to the Black Dragon territory several times and has been the architect of a large-scale World Bank program for aid to China in recuperating from the fire and preventing a new outbreak.

The Chinese won three major programs to help protect and regenerate the Black Dragon Forest. The first was the practical, small Canadian program, which had been in the field since 1985 and was well under way before the terrible day of May 6, 1987. The second was a flat-out, no-strings, one-time-only West German grant of 30 million deutsche marks. This could be used for any purpose the Chinese wished. And most important was the $550 million World Bank loan and grant, providing $50 million from the bank to China and a $500 million commitment from China.

From these international support programs China fashioned a comprehensive forest-protection and re-generation scheme, doubling the size of its fire-prevention service. It provided for the installation of electronic fire detectors, lightning detectors, and alarm systems over the total area of the Black Dragon Forest, including its Mongolian segment — an area roughly the size of Great Britain. Nineteen new observation towers were put in, bringing the total to forty-four, with more to come. Perhaps they didn't need that many, but better too many than too few.

A modern communications system was also in the works. Up to now observers had not even had a pair of field glasses, no proper maps to help fix fire coordinates, no communications at all. They had had to run down from a watchtower, then walk or bicycle sometimes six hours to make a report. Now response time would improve. Response time to a fire is everything. Sometimes it had taken two or three days to get to the site of a fire.

To support the fire-detection program the Chinese purchased a fleet of scooper planes, forestry-type helicopters, lightweight observation, and jumper planes of the kind favored by the Canadians. The planes are far cheaper to operate than the heavy, badly designed fleet of the Civil Aviation Administration of China. It was not clear whether the forestry fleet would be operated by forestry pilots or whether Chinese bureaucracy would compel the Forest Service to use CAAC pilots, subject to complicated, delay-causing, cost-inefficient procedures.

A large segment of the World Bank money was earmarked for replanting. The replanting began in the summer of 1987 at the insistence of Premier Li Peng. But unexpected difficulties emerged. China did not have seed or saplings on the enormous scale required. No major reserves of larch seed, it developed, were available anywhere in the world. The Chinese needed 550,000 pounds of seed. They asked the Soviet Union, but Moscow replied it could not help. It had no large-scale stocks.

American and Canadian specialists had some doubts about so large a planting program. They felt that the losses would be heavy, perhaps up to two thirds of saplings planted. They also warned that planting such large new forests of larch risked the possibility of mass infestation or disease. But the Chinese were going ahead with the program to the limit of their resources, trying to coordinate it with a vast cut of slightly damaged and slightly burned timber.

The cutting program was a central feature of the postfire operation. With World Bank funds the Chinese launched an effort to salvage about 15 million cubic yards of scorched timber — about $1 billion worth at local Chinese prices (it would be worth much more delivered to a U.S. port).

Less than one year after the end of the Black Dragon fire there was great skepticism about how well this program could be carried out. The Chinese did not have facilities to cut, ship, or store so much lumber. They were attempting the largest logging operation ever undertaken in the world — 1.1 million cubic yards in 1987, 4.5 million in 1988, 6.5 million in 1989, and 3 million in 1990.

But the cut did not achieve that pace. Moreover, it was certain before 1987 was out that the logs would have to be cut even faster because decay was advancing more rapidly than had been calculated. The Chinese press was filled with reports of dire danger. The burned stands, already attacked by pests and disease, had to be cut by 1990.

Unfortunately, there was no way to do this. To move this huge bulk of lumber required doubling the capacity of the not too well built railroad, including its limited number of flatcars and locomotives; replacing bridges and culverts; and expanding tunnels, loading platforms, and signal systems. By mid-1988 it was apparent that the salvage operation would probably not reach 50 percent of its target. All through that year estimates of the cut went down and estimates of the overall timber loss went up and up. Only trees of a diameter of ten to twenty inches were being cut. The rest were abandoned in the forest.

An extension of the Tahe-Mohe railroad spur went slowly. Workers were increasing its capacity from 200 million to 400 million tons per year and its trackage from six hundred to twelve hundred miles. Highways were being built more slowly, and the truck fleet was not being expanded materially. Trucking logs was deemed too expensive (the roads were not in very good shape either, being too poor to bear heavy loads). The plan was to move 85 percent of the cut by rail, 3 percent by truck, and the rest by water. There was not enough storage capacity for the logs, so they would be put into rivers and streams and kept underwater, a good preservative because of the high pitch content of the larch.

Another problem was that there simply weren't enough loggers. The forest administration refused to bring in loggers from outside. It insisted on employing the personnel of existing forest farms, plus some workers brought in from the farms of the Lesser Hinggan Forest. They had, they said, twenty thousand men in the woods. No way to get more. The limitation on recruitment was based not on fear of increasing the risk of fire (it goes up exponentially the more people there are in the forest) but primarily on maintaining the stability of the forest family and its unparalleled iron rice bowl.

Eighteen months after the fire there was considerable pessimism among foreign specialists. They contended that the fire and its aftermath had generated extraordinary political and bureaucratic pressures within the forest establishment. Action was subject to agonizing waits while political clearances were obtained. Many bureaucrats simply refused to take any action until someone higher up had vetted it. No one wanted his head to roll.

Everyone kept looking over his shoulder. Everyone recognized that the mass of activity increased the danger of inadvertent starting of new fires: the more men at work, the greater the risk. The replanting program also required more workers than usual, and officials were hoping that a larger workforce would speed the process (it didn't). Every other newspaper was filled with exhortations: The danger of fire! Be on guard! Be alert! China could not afford more losses.

There were few fires in the spring and summer of 1988, largely because of good spring moisture. But one serious fire broke out in North Korea close to the Chinese border. It blazed up to the Chinese line, crossed over, but then petered out, to the relief of the Chinese forest administration.

The most critical part of the new program will be the initial years — 1988–91, the years in which the massive cutting and transportation of timber take place, the years when the enormous replanting is done and all the new equipment goes on-line. These years of great activity are years of great hazard. Defenses are not in place, and hazards are increased by larger numbers of people in the forest zone, people who are unskilled and untrained in the ways of the forest and its dangers.

The challenge is to avert the peril of new fires, another conflagration or series of fires. The alternative is swifter desertification. The example of desertification lies literally next door to the Black Dragon country, easy to see, easy to study. The Gobi has marched across Mongolia to lap at the edges of the forest. The desert has claimed the loesslands of Shaanxi and Shanxi for its own. The emergency shelterbelts of the mass plantings of the Cultural Revolution years have not halted the winds. The death rate of the new saplings has been astronomical.

Each year China is losing 800 square miles to the desert. It has lost nearly 10,000 square miles since 1950. By the year 2000 it will have lost another 10,000. The sand oceans are moving inexorably closer to Manchuria. Nothing now contemplated for the Black Dragon seems likely to stop this relentless parade.

Today in Northwest China there are fifty days a year of sandstorms, a month and a half of blinding grit propelled by endless gales. Another two hundred days are classified as "sandy, dusty." Spring 1988 may have given Beijing a hint of the past that will be its future.

Fifty years ago Captain Hans Koester, a German aviator who flew North and Northeast China for German, Chinese, and American airlines in the 1930s (he spent four thousand hours in flight over China), set down his observations. A German forester who he knew had spent a lifetime trying to reforest the barren lands adjacent to Manchuria.

"To flyers," he wrote, "it is evident that North China is becoming more and more a desert from lack of trees and improvident cultivation."

He described the Gobi as slowly creeping eastward across China in the path of vanishing forests. He told of the large areas of villages, once populated, surrounded with fertile croplands, now destroyed and vacant because of the advance of sand and wind across the treeless plains.

Year by year the remorseless advance continues.

What will be the ecological effect of the world's greatest fire? How will it affect nature, climate, and man?

This is the big question, one too large for a quick or positive reply, a question so profound that no American ecologist is yet prepared to hazard an answer. There are too many ifs.

But it is a question that has come swiftly to the fore, especially with the 1988 Yellowstone fire, which suddenly transfixed American and international attention. The image of one of the world's most famous wilderness preserves devastated by raging fires that, like the Black Dragon's, sent plumes of smoke hundreds of feet into the air — smoke that soon could be perceived by the nostrils of New Yorkers — remarkably focused attention.

The Black Dragon smoke plume appeared over Alaska on May 10, 1987 — less than three days after Xilinji was destroyed. It lowered temperatures by four degrees Fahrenheit. A vast fire is the only force that releases carbon dioxide into the atmosphere in such astronomical quantities. Such scientists as Alan Robock are examining these effects as analogous to nuclear winter. Others are studying Black Dragon for its contribution to the greenhouse effect, which could heat the planet beyond habitation as we know it now. We may freeze, we may burn. We may do both.

It is becoming apparent to millions that these immense fires could incalculably damage the ecosphere, not only the lands over which they burned but the climate itself, and could possibly contribute to the growing danger of destruction of the ozone layer, particularly if the deadly cycle of burn, burn, and burn again should set in.

To some memories leapt the chilling words of the Apocalypse:

> The angel took the censer and filled it with fire of the altar, and cast it into the earth and there were voices and thunderings, and lightnings. . . . and there followed hail and fire mingled with blood . . . and the third part of trees was burnt up, and all green grass was burnt up. . . . and as it were a great mountain burning with fire was cast into the sea.